INTARSIA
WOODWORKING PROJECTS

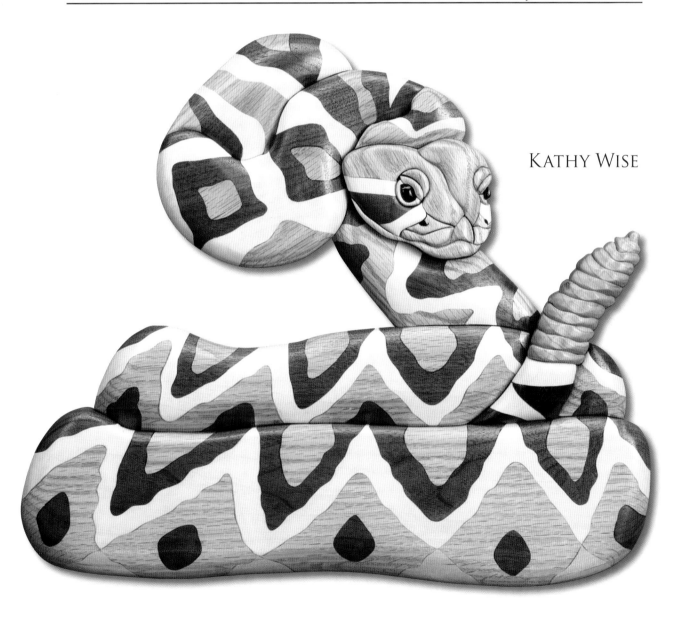

KATHY WISE

FOX CHAPEL
PUBLISHING

ISBN 978-1-56523-339-3

Publisher's Cataloging-in-Publication Data

Wise, Kathy.
      Intarsia woodworking projects : 21 original designs with full-size
      plans and expert instruction for all skill levels / Kathy Wise. -- East
      Petersburg, PA : Fox Chapel Publishing, c2007.

          p. ; cm.

          ISBN: 978-1-56523-339-3

          1. Marquetry. 2.Wood-carving--Patterns. 3. Wildlife woodcarving--
Patterns. I. Title. II. Woodworking projects.

TT192 .W57 2007
745.51/2--dc22   0711

A *Scroll Saw Woodworking & Crafts* magazine publication.

To learn more about the other great books from
Fox Chapel Publishing, or to find a retailer near you,
call toll-free 800-457-9112 or visit us at *www.FoxChapelPublishing.com*.

Note to Authors: We are always looking for talented
authors to write new books. Please send a brief letter describing your idea to
Acquisition Editor, 1970 Broad Street, East Petersburg, PA 17520.

Printed in China
Fourth printing

Table of Contents

Getting Started 1

Beginner Projects

Rose Demonstration 10

Ornaments 18

Penguin & Chick 22

Fox 26

Intermediate Projects

Mallard Demonstration 30

Love Birds 40

Piano Girls 42

Pool Balls 48

Lighthouse 50

Sailboat 52

Advanced Projects

Lion Demonstration 54

Rattlesnake 64

Barn Scene 66

Calf Roper 68

Clydesdale and Colt.. 70

Eagle.. 72

INTRODUCTION

INTARSIA: THE WISE WAY

Intarsia is an early Italian art, a form of wood inlay. Over time, it evolved into a more sculptural style of wood art. Each intarsia artist has his or her own technique and approach to the art.

I believe there is no wrong way to create intarsia, just different styles. Don't be hampered by the "rules" of intarsia. There are none. Feel free to change the patterns. Add exotic woods or other materials such as glass, stone, or plastic. Use stains, paints, oils, or dyes to enhance the colors and achieve the look you want. Add as much depth as possible to your project; make it jump out at you.

I have seen some wonderful versions of my designs embellished with feathers, glass, and color dyes. In other words, the pattern is just a starting point, a guide for your own special brand of artistic creativity. Make it into your own masterpiece.

Having sculpted animals and dogs for more than 30 years, I like to add as much 3D-effect to my intarsia as possible. The color of the wood is important, as well as the light and dark values used in the design.

Whether you are an old pro or a beginning intarsia artist, this book has something for everyone. It will help you to learn the basics or improve your skills. Patterns range from beginner to intermediate to advanced, along with some step-by-step photos and instructions mixed in with helpful advice.

With careful selection, you can create beautiful contrasts using only natural wood colors.

NATURAL WOOD VS. STAIN/PAINT

I prefer to use the natural wood colors in most of my projects, but sometimes a project requires an unavailable or impossible-to-find color. For example: the head of my turkey needed to be blue to really look like a turkey, so I applied a light wash of acrylic paint to the bird's-eye maple, which gave me the light blue color.

There is some debate as to whether you should alter the wood with stains, dyes, or paint. Think of the finished artwork—will using stains, paints, or dyes enhance your piece? Using white gel stain on white wood is widely accepted by intarsia artists. I fail to see any difference in using washes or dyes on your pieces, as long as you allow the wood grain to show through as much as possible. Using stains and washes allows you to use available woods without the expense of the exotic woods.

It often depends upon the effect you are looking to achieve. I used acrylic paint washes on the *Pool Ball* project featured in the intermediate section. You will notice that the wood grain still shows through. The pool balls would not have been realistic enough for me if they were the natural color of the wood. That particular project would also be an ideal situation to experiment with colored plastics.

Some woods can darken or lighten with age. To keep black walnut very dark, I use a dark walnut oil on it to preserve and enrich the deep brown color. I use white gel stain on my white pieces in order to keep the wood from turning brown with age. See the section on finishing for more details on applying white gel stain.

Some projects, such as *Pool Balls,* require the use of paints or dyes to achieve the correct colors.

EQUIPMENT

Some artists cut their work entirely with a hand fret saw. An investment in a few basic tools will really increase the efficiency of your work and your enjoyment.

There are many brands of scroll saws available. If you plan to spend a lot of time scrolling, I recommend you invest in a higher-end saw.

THE SCROLL SAW

The thin blades of a scroll saw allow you to make straight and curved cuts and even 180° turns with no difficulty. If you do not already own a scroll saw and plan on doing large projects, pick a saw that has a large throat depth and a large table. Variable speed is also useful. As with any tool, buy the best that you can afford. If possible, visit a store or woodworking show where you can actually try out the different brands before making a purchase. Ask other woodworkers for their input, but be aware that opinions on saws vary as greatly as opinions on the make and model of automobiles. Being able to "test-drive" the saw is always your best option.

When you get the saw set up, position a chair at a comfortable height and get familiar with the saw. Check to see how the blades are clamped in the machine and check to make sure the blade is square to the table. You can tilt the table of your saw to cut the wood at an angle, which can produce some interesting results. However, for intarsia, you almost always want the blade to be square to the table. Otherwise, your pieces will not fit together properly. Check that the blade is square to the table both front to back and side to side. Then figure out how to tension your blade; in most cases, the blade should be tight enough that it moves less than ⅛" side-to-side when you press on it.

Next, check your scrolling environment. Make sure you have adequate light, and have some method of cleaning the air (a dust mask at the very least). Make some marks on a piece of scrap wood and try cutting. If you want to jump right into a project, mark the outside edges of the design with a highlighter; you do not need to be quite as careful when cutting those lines. Cut slowly, and stay on your lines. Most of all practice, practice, practice; your skills will improve with each cut.

BASIC TOOLS

To create intarsia, it is best to have access to the following tools. While they are not all absolutely necessary, having them will speed up the process and make the process more enjoyable.
- Scroll saw
- Pneumatic drum sander
- Small die grinder or rotary power carver such as a Dremel with a ½"-diameter sanding drum
- Air cleaner
- Drill press
- Sanding mop
- Band saw
- Woodburner
- Clamps and/or sand bags

OTHER TOOLS

While you won't get quite as much use out of the following tools, you will find them very helpful. If you plan to undertake intarsia on a serious level, I strongly advise you to invest in these items.
- Dust collection system
- Table saw
- Router & assorted bits
- Belt sander
- Oscillating sander
- Planer
- Finishing sander
- Circular saw

SUPPLIES

These relatively inexpensive items are available at most craft or hardware stores and will be essential additions to your shop.
- Carving knife or hobby knife
- Sandpaper
- Needle nose pliers/forceps
- Gel varnish/spray varnish
- Dust mask
- Contact paper
- Spray adhesive
- Double-stick carpet tape
- Clear packing tape
- Glue stick

Use a small square to make sure your blade is square to the table.

BLADES

There are two main types of blades for the scroll saw: plain-end and pin-end. Pin-end blades have a small pin in the end that locks into the blade holders; plain-end blades do not have this pin. Plain-end blades come in smaller sizes and more varieties; they are the blades used in this book. Most saws are equipped to receive plain-end blades which come in a wide variety of styles and sizes.

Basic styles: With **reverse-tooth blades** the bottom 5-7 teeth are reversed (point upwards). Since these teeth come up into the workpiece, they leave a clean edge on the bottom of the piece. They tend to force some sawdust back into the cut, so they should not be used to cut hard, dense wood. On **skip-tooth blades** every other tooth is eliminated. This helps to remove the chips and sawdust more effectively, making it easier to cut hard, dense wood, or wood that burns easily. These blades leave a burr on the bottom of the wood that must be sanded off. **Regular-tooth blades** feature evenly spaced teeth that all run in the same direction. They cut slower but smoother than skip-tooth blades, and they will also leave a burr on the bottom of the wood.

Sizes: In addition to the style of blade, blades come in a variety of sizes. Generally, the lower the number, the smaller the blade. Higher number blades cut more aggressively. I recommend a #3 or smaller blade for pieces with sharp turns, small details, or for soft or thin wood. Use it for cutting larger sections into smaller pieces; it will have a smaller kerf (amount of material that is cut away),

and your pieces will fit together better. Use a #5 or #7 for harder or thicker wood and for cutting outside edges (edges that will not be fitted next to another piece). Your best bet is to get a large variety of different sizes and types and try them out on your wood. Every intarsia artist has a favorite blade. I like the Polar Skip-Tooth blades for their ease of cutting through hard, thick woods, but I will switch to a reverse-tooth blade for lauan or thin wood.

EQUIPMENT DOS AND DON'TS

DO:
- Know your scroll saw and be comfortable using it.
- Experiment with assorted blades to find the kind you like best for the type of wood you are cutting.
- Square your blade and check your tension often.
- Back off the blade and turn your wood for sharp curves.
- Take your time; it is not a race. Have patience.
- Cut out each wood section first, then cut them into smaller pieces with a smaller blade.
- Cut smaller pieces from the large piece first; this will give you more to hold on to.
- Split the line with your blade as you cut.
- Correct your mistakes gradually; if you wander off a line, ease back on to it.
- Wear a face mask and have a good dust collection system in place; many woods produce toxic dust.
- Have a comfortable chair and have it adjusted to the correct height to eliminate back strain.
- Replace your blades often; when you have to start pushing more on your wood, it's time to change.
- Have good lighting to help cut down on eye strain.
- Use a piece of sandpaper to clean the ends of your new blade each time you change them; it will remove the machining oil and dirt and prevent slipping from the blade holders.
- Number all your pieces on the bottom with a pencil for easy placement and so you don't accidentally sand the wrong side.

DON'T:
- Push the wood too quickly; let the blade cut the wood.
- Push to the side; this will cause the blade to bend and make a good fit difficult.
- Use wood that is not flat; it will vibrate when you cut and result in uneven side cuts.
- Be intimated by any project; if it doesn't come out the first time like you think it should, try again.

Using the copy and paste method, I group the pieces by color and then attach them to the wood.

PATTERN LAYOUT

Keep in mind the pattern is just a starting point for your intarsia work of art. It is a guide and is not written in stone. Feel free to change color or grain direction, and add or leave out pieces to make it your own personal creation.

There are several methods to transfer your pattern onto the wood. Experiment to determine which method you like the best.

PATTERN TRANSFER METHODS

Copy and paste: Make several copies of your pattern pieces and use spray adhesive to adhere the copies to the wood. It is the fastest and easiest method for me.

Carbon paper tracing: Use carbon paper under your pattern and trace each piece onto the wood.

Trace edges and fit: After each piece is cut, lay it next to the adjoining pattern piece and retrace your cutting line for a tight fit.

THE COPY AND PASTE METHOD

Make several copies of the pattern, up to 6 or 7 depending on how many pieces are in the project. Then cut apart each piece and group them into colors of wood. I spray the back of the pattern pieces and adhere them to the shiny side of contact paper. I use Con-Tact Brand contact paper. Cut the pieces apart. Peel and stick your pattern pieces to the wood. You can also cover your board with clear packing tape and then adhere the pattern.

I use the pattern glued to the contact paper because it will peel off easily without leaving a gummy glue residue on the wood. It also lubricates the blade and helps prevent some woods, like cherry, from burning when you cut. I often change my mind when positioning patterns, and the contact paper is easy to peel off and reapply. Pay special attention to the direction of the grain and align your pattern pieces accordingly.

PATTERN DOS AND DON'TS

DO:
- Save a master copy of your pattern for future use.
- Make enough copies for all the pieces to be cut apart.
- Make all your copies from one copier; otherwise you may have distortions.
- Mark your outside edges with a highlighter; you can be less strict about staying on those lines.
- Use the grain direction arrows, but don't feel locked into using them if an interesting grain pattern "fits" the piece just right.
- Use a good-quality spray adhesive.
- Move your pattern around the board looking for good areas, and consider flipping the board over for more options.
- Use name brand contact paper. I recommend Con-Tact Brand clear contact paper.
- Keep a full copy glued to the backing board to position your pieces on as you cut.
- Make sure your wood is dust free before sticking the pattern pieces onto it.
- Keep clear tape handy when cutting in case your pattern starts flapping from not enough glue; it also works well to use over the paper pattern edges when cutting dense or oily exotic woods where your pattern wants to slip.
- Trim your paper pattern pieces close to the edge so you can fit them closely on the wood if needed.

DON'T:
- Have any parts of your pattern overhanging the wood; trim it tight to the edge.
- Let overspray from the adhesive float around; spray the adhesive into a large box or spray it outside.
- Disregard new methods to do things without first trying them; keep an open mind and you may be surprised.

Careful selection of color and grain will enhance your project.

WOOD SELECTION

The availability of many different species of wood is one of the things that makes intarsia such an exciting art form. All the patterns have color codes to indicate the shade of wood to use: W=white, B=black, D=dark, MD=medium dark, M=medium, ML=medium light, L=light, and R=reddish shade.

Since some wood will have both light and dark areas, it is up to the intarsia artist to select the colors. Keep in mind you want contrasting colors and values. If you keep to one color/species of wood, your piece will turn out monotone and dull.

Use the blackest wood you can for the eyes. This will make your piece pop. I buy ebony scraps in a bulk package whenever possible. I cut them into ½"-thick pieces for my eyes and shim them up to the level I need. Black walnut and wenge are great dark woods. I use poplar, aspen, or cottonwood for my white areas. Cherry, beech, and mahogany are nice colors for medium tones. Ash and maple are good light colors. Lay out assorted varnished scraps of wood onto your pattern to get a feel for the colors and tones you will be using. By varnishing the scraps, you'll get a better feel for the true end color. Step back and see how the colors stand up at a distance—that is how you will be viewing the finished project.

Next check your wood for interesting grain patterns and knots. Avoid grains with a lot of light and dark variations, such as zebra wood. Unless it is used to draw attention to a special area, it tends to detract from your overall design by making your eye go straight to that area and not to the entire piece. Sky and water areas are great places to use a spalted, burled, or highly figured wood.

EXOTIC VS. DOMESTIC WOODS

Most of the wood I use has been cut here in Michigan on our own property. A portable saw mill makes short work of the large logs. I use cherry, poplar, beech, ash, hickory, black walnut, maple, oak, and cedar. I like to put a splash of color in some of my pieces with a bit of exotic wood. I use it sparingly and/or only for special projects. Some of this wood is expensive and may be hard to find, so consider using a light stain or wash to get nearly the same effect. As long as you allow the grain to show through and the color is not too intense, it can be made to look natural. Many exotic scraps are available through flooring companies.

SANDING TOOLS

There are many different tools available to contour and shape your work. The method you use depends on personal preference as well as availability. It is possible to achieve beautiful results with nothing more than sandpaper and elbow grease. While the hand sanding method is the most inexpensive, it does require a large commitment of time. Due to space constraints, I'll only address the three main types that I use in this section.

I use coarse sandpaper on the larger drum and remove scratches with a finer grit on the small drum.

PNEUMATIC DRUM SANDER

I use a pneumatic drum sander for 95% of all my sanding. Because it has an air-filled bladder inside of a canvas sleeve covered by sandpaper, it will give slightly when you push your wood against it. This enables you far more control when shaping, and is faster than a belt sander, oscillating sander, and many other sanding methods. I always use rubber finger tips to protect my fingers from being sanded as well. They come in many sizes and are available at most office supply stores.

My sander has two drums. On the 8" diameter drum, I put 100-grit sandpaper to remove wood quickly. The other drum has a 2" diameter, and I have 180-grit sandpaper on it to remove the scratches from the rougher grit, and put a nice finish on the pieces. I sand pieces as small as ¼" x ¼" using pliers or tweezers to hold the pieces.

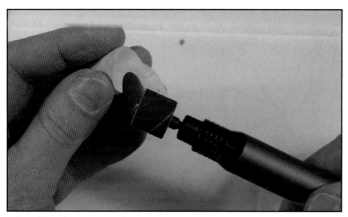

A hand-held rotary tool lets you shape hard-to-reach areas.

SMALL GRINDER/ ROTARY POWER CARVER

For inside edges or hard-to-reach areas, I use an air grinder or rotary power carver with a ¼"-diameter or ½"-diameter sanding drum. It puts a nice, smooth finish on the wood before I move on to the sanding mop.

A sanding mop speeds up the final polishing and finishing step.

SANDING MOP

While you can hand sand every piece with fine-grit sandpaper, I use a sanding mop for the finishing stage. It saves so much time and effort. You get a beautiful polished finish in an instant.

I have two mops mounted on a variable-speed grinder. Variable speed is almost a must, because some wood will burn at the higher speeds. I use a 120-grit mop first, which removes the sharp edges of the wood, and then I move on to a 220-grit mop to finish sand the pieces.

HAND SANDING

To hand sand any small crevices that the mop can't get to, I use a piece of rolled-up sandpaper. Cut lines can be sanded by feeding a small strip of sandpaper back and forth through the cut. Cheap emery nail file boards in various grits work wonderfully for sanding and are available in most discount stores.

SANDING & SHAPING

Creating different levels within your piece is what brings an intarsia project to life. Most projects are cut from wood that is 1" thick or less. Achieving the illusion of depth within that limited space can take some practice.

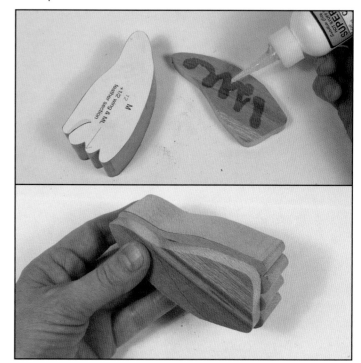

Use CA glue to attach risers to individual pieces. Be sure to cut the riser slightly smaller than the intarsia piece.

SHIMMING UP LEVELS

Position the cut pieces on your full pattern sheet. Look over the piece and see where the shims are indicated on the pattern. If none are indicated, see if you have any areas that can be raised to give more depth to your piece. I use ¼"-½"-thick risers or shims. You can use plywood or scrap wood that is the right thickness. Cut just inside the area you want raised. On small pieces, the shims can be glued to the bottom. As you sand, make sure the shims are in place on your assembled project to make sure you do not sand the pieces next to the shim too low and expose the shim.

SHAPING CONTOURS

Start by marking your wood where you want to remove material. Sand small amounts of wood away, put it back in place, and check it in relation to the other pieces. You may have to replace and sand each piece as many as 8 to 10 times. Be patient; as you gain experience in sanding, you will be able to judge how much to take off, and your sanding time will go down. Once the wood is gone, it is gone, and you can't put it back, so go slowly.

Sand each piece in small increments and replace it often to check progress.

Sanding Shims & Spot Gluing

There are a few ways to sand pieces together. Take the neck of a horse, for example. You want to sand the three pieces together as one so you have a nice flowing contour to the entire section. Then you can take them apart and sand each piece a bit more.

Shim and double-sided tape: Make a sanding shim by tracing your pieces on to a piece of scrap plywood. Cut it out and attach the pieces to the shim with double-sided tape. This will support your pieces as one until you are done shaping. This method is time consuming, since you will have to make a sanding shim for every section you sand as one.

Spot glue with cyanoacrylate (CA) glue: This is my favorite method; it's very fast and easy and I use it 90% of the time. Put two or three small dots of CA glue (I use Instant T Glue) near the bottom of one side of your two pieces. Spray the wood with accelerator, and fit the two together on top of a very flat surface covered with paper. As you are holding it together, rotate it as it dries to prevent it from sticking to the paper. It will only take about 15 seconds to dry completely, so you have to work quickly. Add on other parts one at a time. Now your piece is glued together and you can sand the contours you wish to shape as one continuous piece. To take the pieces apart, simply rap the pieces on a hard surface, and they will break apart. Practice on some scrap wood before you try it out. Don't use this method with small, fragile, or delicate pieces. Once you get comfortable using this method, you may never make another sanding shim.

Carving Details

You may have to do a little light carving in places where you can't use an air grinder tool. A good carving knife is a great tool to have. A hobby knife with a new blade can be a workable alternative.

Woodburning Details

Use a woodburner to add small details to your intarsia. Some areas, like an eye on a small piece, can be burned in instead of cut. Stitching on the saddle area of the *Calf Roper* project featured in the advanced section was done with a woodburner. It adds a lot of interest very quickly. Practice on scrap wood before you jump right into your project.

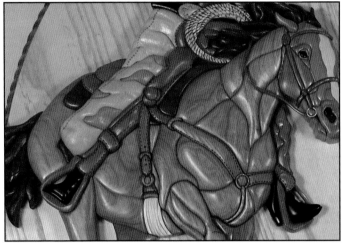
Use a woodburner to add small details, such as the stitching on the saddle area of *Calf Roper*.

Sanding Dos and Don'ts

DO:
- Use risers whenever possible to give more depth and dimension to your project; put them in place before you start shaping.
- Have a work table on rollers that you can move from your saw to sander easily.
- Wear rubber finger tips when using the sanding drum; they will save your fingers.
- Peel off the pattern before you sand.
- Wear eye protection.
- Wear a face mask and have a good dust collection system in place; many woods have toxic dust.
- Sand with the grain whenever possible.
- Slowly take off the wood to your marked levels, replace the piece back next to the other pieces, and remark until you are at the right level; you may have to repeat several times for one area.
- Use CA glue to hold pieces together for sanding; it's much quicker than using a sanding shim.

DON'T:
- Let your riser show by sanding the areas next to it too low.
- Remove wood too fast; you can't put it back.
- Be afraid of sanding; if you do remove too much wood and your piece is ruined, all you have to do is re-cut another piece, and sand it again.

APPLYING A FINISH

Finishing not only protects your project, but also brings out the natural colors of your wood. It's important to know what effect your finish will have and I recommend you test the finish on your wood before applying to the completed project.

WHITE GEL STAIN

To keep white pieces from turning yellow or brown, use white gel stain. Make sure your pieces are dust and dirt free before you apply the white gel stain. Follow the manufacturer's directions. Apply a coat of white gel stain with a rag or brush and let it set for a few minutes. Then wipe it off and let it dry for 6–12 hours. When dry, apply a second coat, using the same technique. Let the stain dry overnight.

Gel varnish can be applied to each individual piece or after the intarsia has been assembled.

GEL VARNISH

I use two methods for applying the gel depending upon the intarsia piece.

Method #1: Wipe each piece with gel varnish before you glue the intarsia together. Apply two coats of gel varnish on each piece, coating the top and sides. Let it set a few minutes, wipe it off, and let it dry overnight between each coat.

Method #2: Wipe the varnish onto the glued-together intarsia and blow off the excess. It is much quicker than varnishing every little piece. Wipe a coat of gel varnish on with a rag, and use a brush to get into the cracks and small areas. Wipe off as much as you can with a rag. Use an air gun or an air compressor to blow the excess gel varnish out of the cracks and wipe it again with the rag. Use a cotton swab to get into the small areas. Let it dry overnight before applying a second coat using the same technique.

Because *Calf Roper* contains so many small pieces, I apply the finish after the project is assembled.

SPRAY VARNISH

On an intarsia piece that has a lot of small pieces and details, like *Calf Roper*, I use a satin spray varnish. It covers well and is easy to apply. Follow the manufacturer's directions.

ASSEMBLY

Most intarsia artists have a preferred assembly method. Some use CA or wood glue to join the pieces; some glue the individual pieces directly onto the backing board. I prefer to tack the pieces before I secure the assembled project to the backing board.

Tack sections together with a few drops of 100% silicone glue.

SILICONE TACKING

I use 100% silicone glue or caulk (they are the same thing) to tack the pieces together before I glue them to the backing board. Position the pieces on the pattern and tack the sections together with two or three small dots of silicone. Be sure to follow the pattern carefully. Don't apply too much glue; you don't want the silicone to push up through the seams. Let the glue dry overnight. When you go to glue the piece to the backing board with wood glue, your pieces will stay in the correct place. If you have to break it apart to adjust a piece, it will do so easily. For larger projects, divide it into a few smaller sections, and tack them together.

GLUING

Apply a good-quality wood glue evenly to the clean backing board. Place the tacked-together project onto the board, and clamp or weigh it down with sandbags. Let the glue dry overnight. You can also use a quick-setting epoxy.

INSTALLING A HANGER

Hold your project between two fingers to find the balance point. Mark and drill a hole for your hanger. Be sure not to drill all the way through to the front of your piece. Mirror hangers work well. For heavier pieces, I find the balance point and add two screw eyes level with the balance point. Then string heavy picture wire between the two screw eyes. This is a strong and easy way to hang your piece level.

FINISHING DO'S AND DON'TS

DO:

- Use a sanding mop to put a finished polish on your pieces.
- Use a woodburner to add small details; practice on a scrap piece first.
- Glue some small pieces together as you work.
- Hand sand areas that are hard to get to; nail emery boards work well for small areas.
- Check your pieces for scratches and bumps, and re-sand those areas.
- Sand off any pencil lines.
- Use gel varnish; it gives you a beautiful finish.
- Use spray varnish if your piece has a lot of small pieces and is glued together.
- Tack together pieces with 100% silicone glue before gluing to the backing board.
- Use a white gel stain to keep your white wood from yellowing when the varnish is applied.
- Use good-quality wood glue or epoxy to attach the intarsia to the backing board.

DON'T:

- Leave the backer board looking tacky; finish the rear of your backing board. Paint or stain the back and around the edges. Be sure the board is not visible from the front. People will notice.
- Let the grain rise up after varnishing, leaving a rough finish. After the varnish is dry, use a brown paper bag or very fine steel wool to rub the surface smooth.
- Drill through your piece when attaching the hanger; measure your depth carefully.

Apply a thin layer of wood glue to the backing board then attach the tacked sections.

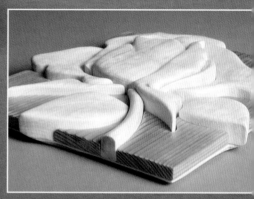

Rose Demonstration

Wood

2 each ½"-⅝" x 9" x 10" contrasting-colored wood
2 each ¼"-⅛" x 9" x 10" lauan plywood or masonite
¼"-thick scrap plywood (riser)

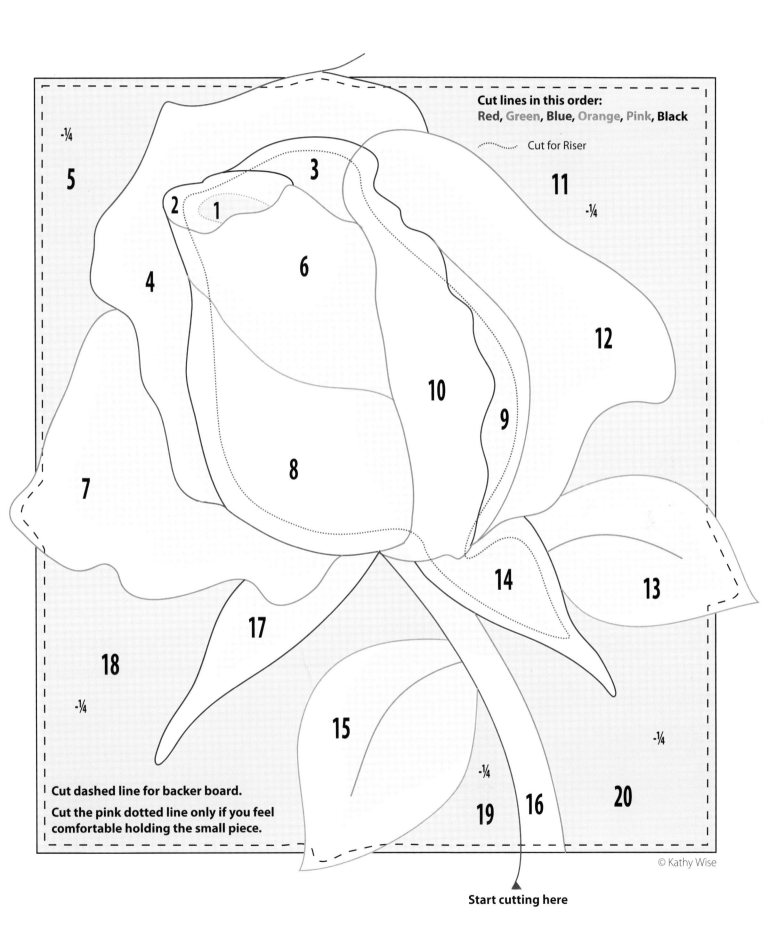

Cut lines in this order:
Red, Green, Blue, Orange, Pink, Black

·········· Cut for Riser

-¼

5

11

-¼

2   1

3

4

6

12

10

9

7

8

14

13

17

18

-¼

15

-¼

-¼

Cut dashed line for backer board.

Cut the pink dotted line only if you feel comfortable holding the small piece.

19   16

20

© Kathy Wise

Start cutting here

Rose Intarsia

This beginner rose is a good exercise to help you learn the fundamentals of cutting and shaping intarsia. This project is stack cut for simplicity. It is important to let the blade cut at its own speed; the harder the wood, the more likely you are to push too hard and bevel the cuts. I recommend a soft wood such as cedar. Always make sure your blade is square to the table before beginning to cut any pieces. When all the pieces are cut, mix and match them for two complete rose projects.

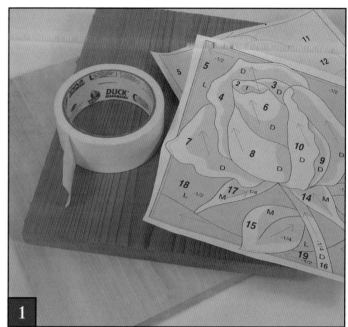

Select two pieces of ⅝"-thick soft wood in contrasting colors. I use a light piece of poplar and a medium shade of cedar. Plane the wood, if needed, to ensure they are the same thickness. Make a practice cut on two scrap pieces of the wood you are using. If it seems too difficult to cut, use thinner pieces. Thinner wood is easier to cut, but prevents you from achieving depth with your shaping.

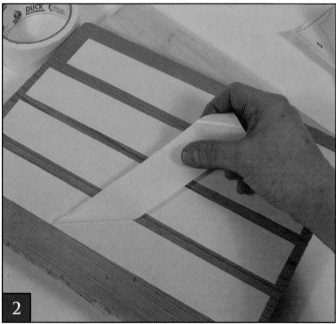

Tape the wood together. Use several pieces of double-sided tape. You can orient the grain of both pieces the same way, or rotate one piece 90°. Tape the edges together with masking tape if they are not tight. Select two pieces of lauan plywood or masonite, and secure them with one strip of double-sided tape for the backing boards.

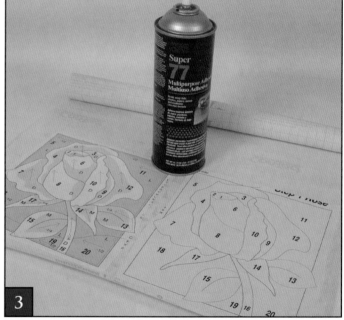

Make two copies of the color-coded pattern. If you cannot make color copies, keep the book close as a reference when you cut out the pieces, or use markers to trace the colored lines onto the pattern. Apply spray adhesive to the back of the patterns. Adhere the patterns onto the shiny side of the contact paper.

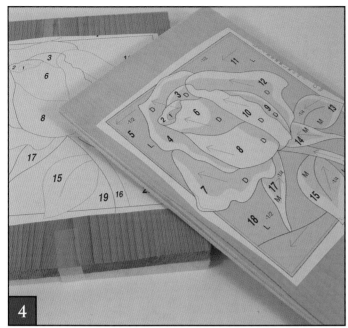

4

Transfer the patterns to the wood stacks. Cut out each pattern piece, remove the backing paper, and stick them to the wood and backing boards. Alternatively, you can cover the stacks of wood with clear packaging tape and adhere the patterns directly to the tape. I prefer the contact paper method, because it enables me to reposition the pattern piece if needed.

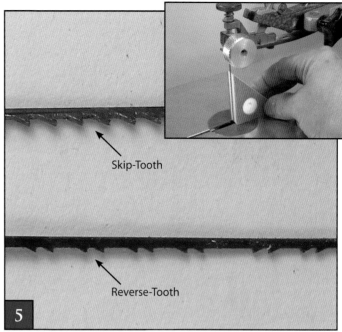

Skip-Tooth

Reverse-Tooth

5

Choose your blade. In addition to your personal preference, the blade you use depends on the type and thickness of the wood you are cutting. I use a #3 or #5 reverse-tooth blade to cut the backing boards. For thick or hard wood such as the stack for the rose, I use a Flying Dutchman #5 Polar Skip-Tooth blade. Make sure your blade is square to the table.

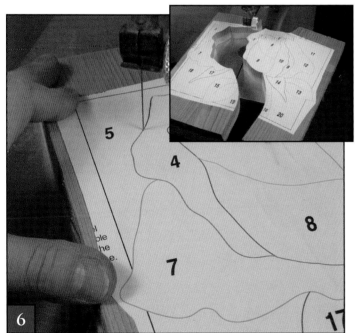

6

Cut the solid red line on the main stack. Cut slowly and let the blade do the work. If you push too fast, you will bend the blade and your bottom pieces will not fit well into your top pieces. If you stray off the line, don't make a sharp correction. Instead, ease back onto the line. Because you are stack cutting, precision cutting is not essential.

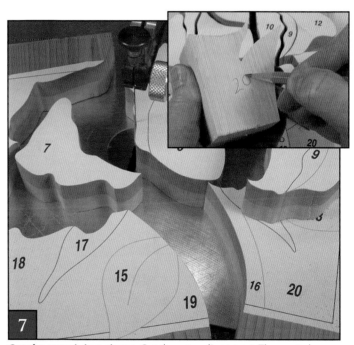

7

Cut the remaining pieces. Cut the green lines next. Then cut along the blue lines. As you cut the pieces, write the numbers on the back of each piece. Sand any burrs off of the bottoms. Continue to cut the pieces following the colored lines in the following order: orange, pink, and then black.

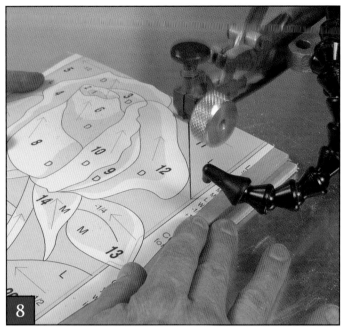

8

Cut the backing boards. Cut along the black dotted line on the pattern. By cutting slightly inside the outer perimeter of the pattern line, you give support to the intarsia piece, but keep the backing board from being visible when the project is completed. Separate the stack, and sand the edges.

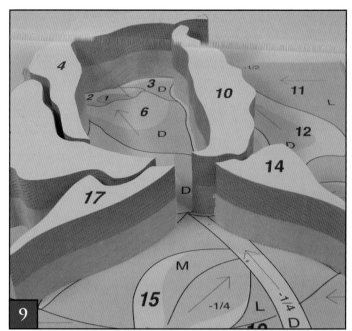

9

Dry assemble the intarsia. Place the cut pieces in position on the backing boards. Use the full pattern as a reference. Remove the paper pattern from the pieces and swap out the contrasting colors on the background pieces so you have one light rose on a dark background and a dark rose on a light background.

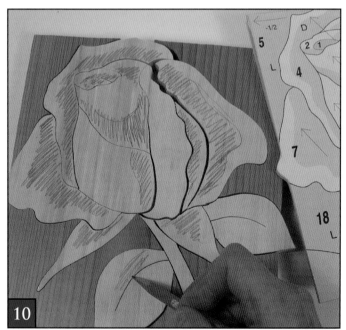

10

Mark the areas to sand and shape. Use a pencil to mark the areas on each piece. Refer to the shaded sanding guide on the pattern and transfer these areas to both sets of pieces. These shaded areas will be sanded down to give depth to the piece.

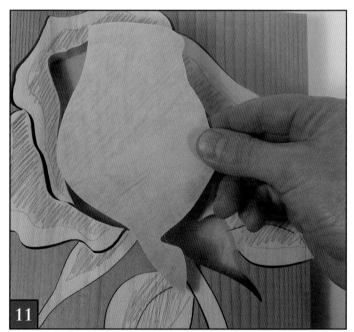

11

Cut a riser for the center of the rose. Sections 1, 2, 3, 6, 8, 9, 10, and 14 will be the highest areas. Use a full pattern to cut a ¼-thick piece of plywood slightly inside the perimeter of the combined section of these pieces. Position the riser under these pieces in the center.

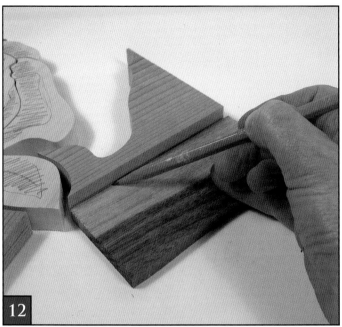

Mark the depth of the background pieces. Use a scrap piece of wood approximately ¼" thick to mark around the perimeter of each background piece. You want to reduce the thickness of the background pieces to make the rose stand out. The pencil lines give you a consistent depth to sand all the background pieces to.

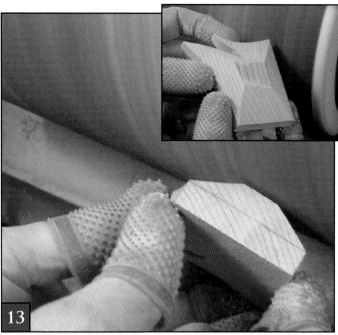

Sand the background pieces. I use a pneumatic drum sander, but you can use your method of choice. I use rubber fingertips to protect my fingers and tweezers or needle-nose pliers to hold the small pieces. Start by sanding the wood down to the lines on all four sides. Then sand the center flat to the lines on the outside.

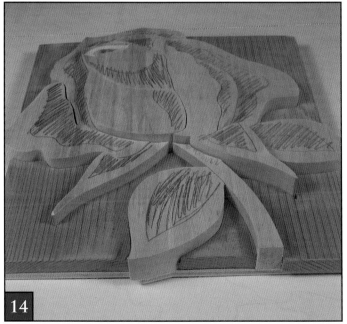

Reposition the background pieces. Replace the pieces back onto the pattern and check the depth. Make sure you have reduced the thickness of all the contrasting background pieces before proceeding. All the background pieces should be level without any dips or valleys.

Shape the stem. Reduce the thickness of the stem and shape it where it meets the rose. Pencil a line indicating the depth you want. If you are unsure, take a little off, replace it onto the pattern, remark and sand a little more off. Shaping is all about marking, sanding, replacing it to the pattern, and repeating the whole process again.

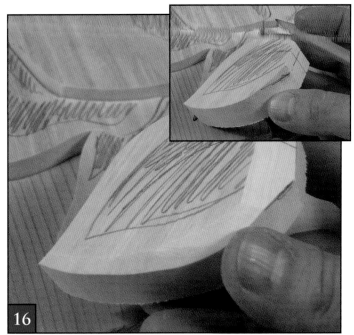

16 **Shape the leaf.** Mark the inside edge of the leaf where it meets the stem and sand down to that level. Maintain the height on the outside edges, rounding them only slightly. Remove wood in small increments. If you remove too much, you can make the piece appear higher by reducing the thickness of the adjoining pieces.

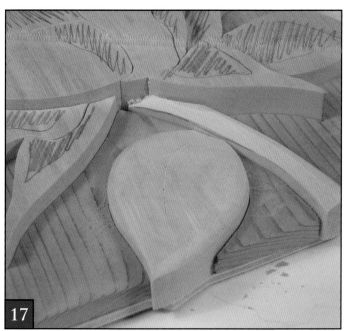

17 **Contour the leaf.** A 2"-diameter sanding drum makes a nice concave slope to the leaf. Round off the entire leaf and leave a smooth surface. Replace the piece next to the other pieces and determine if you have achieved the correct depth in relation to the pieces around it. Repeat the process to shape the other full leaf.

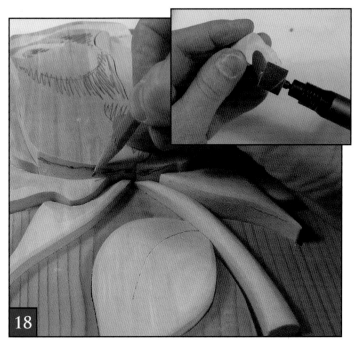

18 **Shape the remaining pieces.** Start with the areas farthest back first. This establishes the lowest level right away and you can build from there. Be careful not to expose the shim by sanding adjoining pieces too much. A handheld rotary tool shapes the smaller pieces.

19 **Check your work.** Replace the pieces to check your levels often. The highest pieces require only minimal rounding of the edges. Position the entire project on the backing board and double check that you are satisfied with the depths and overall look of the piece.

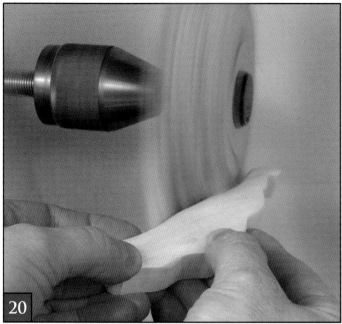

20

Polish the pieces. Give the pieces a final sanding by hand with fine sandpaper or with a sanding mop. If you are using soft wood, make sure your speed is low so you don't burn the wood. Be careful not to sand away the softer sections between the grain lines, which will give you a bumpy surface.

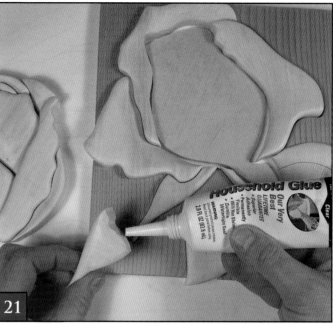

21

Tack the pieces together. Place the pieces on a flat surface. Place the inside riser section in position and work out from there. Put a few drops of 100% silicone glue between each piece and tack the sections together. Don't use too much glue; you do not want it to ooze up between the seams. Allow the silicone to dry overnight.

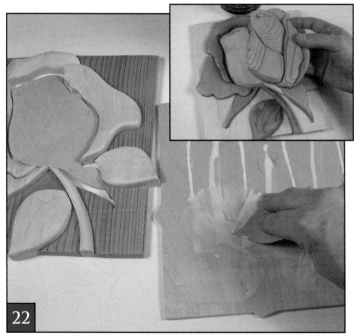

22

Glue the pieces to the backing board. Spread wood glue evenly, but not too thickly, on the backing board. Place the tacked-together outside section and the riser onto the backer board. Then apply glue to the surface of the riser and place the tacked-together middle section of rose onto the riser. Clean up any excess glue with a wet cotton swab.

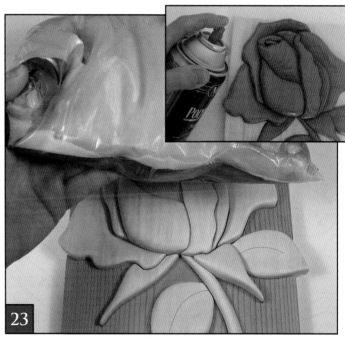

23

Clamp the pieces until the glue dries. Use sandbags or clamp the pieces in place and let the glue dry overnight. Trim any place where the backing board overhangs the pieces and straighten up the outside edges if needed. Spray several coats of varnish on your projects. Attach the saw-tooth hangers to the backs to complete the projects.

Ornaments

Wood½" x 4" x 4" scrap wood for each ornament

Legend
R................ Reddish Shade of Wood
W .... Any White Wood
D .... Dark Shade of Wood
M............... Medium Shade of Wood
ML .... Medium Light Shade
L .... Light Shade of Wood

INTARSIA TIPS

For the green areas, you can stain, dye, or paint the areas lightly so the wood grain shows through, or use lignum vitae, which turns green after it is exposed to sunlight.

If you stack cut an ornament with two different colors, the pieces will fit together perfectly and you will have two complete ornaments.

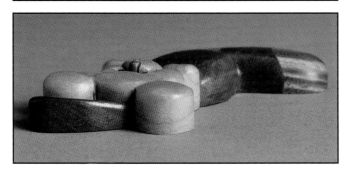

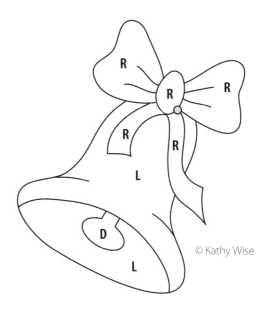

© Kathy Wise

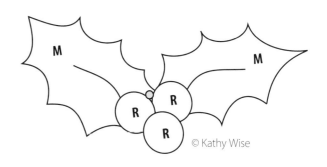

© Kathy Wise

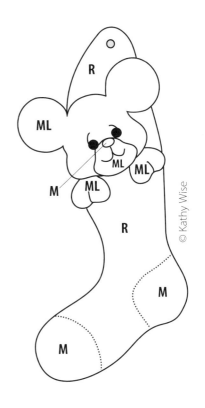

© Kathy Wise

Ornaments

Wood ½" x 4" x 4" scrap wood for each ornament

Legend
R .... Reddish Shade of Wood
W .... Any White Wood
D .... Dark Shade of Wood
M .... Medium Shade of Wood
ML .... Medium Light Shade
L .... Light Shade of Wood

INTARSIA TIPS

Burn the ends of dowel rods or cut small pieces of ebony and insert them into drilled holes for the eyes.

There is no need to add a backing board unless you plan to enlarge the patterns for decorative use.

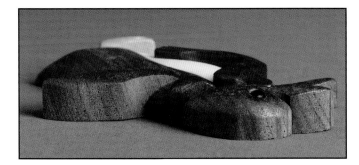

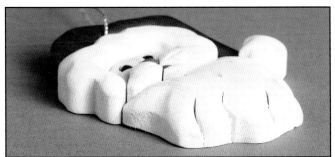

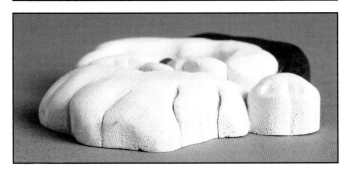

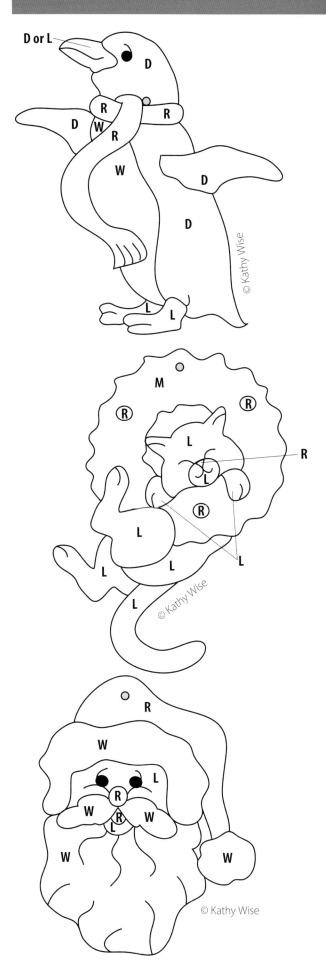

Penguin & Chick

Wood

¾" x 6" x 6" light wood such as yellow pine with gray streaks (chick's body)

¾" x 4" x 4" yellow wood such as yellowheart (yellow patch)

¾" x 2" x 4" orange wood such as goncolo alves, cocobolo, or Austrian cypress (orange patch and beak)

¾" x 9" x 18" dark wood such as black walnut or ebony (body)

¾" x 10" x 14" white wood such as poplar, aspen, or holly (body)

½" x 2" x 1" black wood such as ebony, or your stained/burned wood of choice (eyes)

¾" x 3" x 3" light wood such as maple (chick's face)

¼"-⅛" x 16" x 22" lauan plywood, Baltic birch plywood, or masonite (backing board)

Legend
Start with ¾" wood
——→ Grain Direction
B .... Black/Very Darkest Shade
D .... Dark Shade of Wood
Or .... Orange Shade or Stain
ML .... Medium Light Shade
L .... Light Shade of Wood
W .... Any White Wood
-¼" .... Sand or Plane Down -¼"
+¼" .... Use ¼" Thicker Wood
⌒⌒⌒⌒ Cut for Riser

INTARSIA TIPS

Glue the light section of the chick's head inside the dark section before shaping.

Use a stain or dye for the orange and yellow areas if you can't find a wood that is naturally that color.

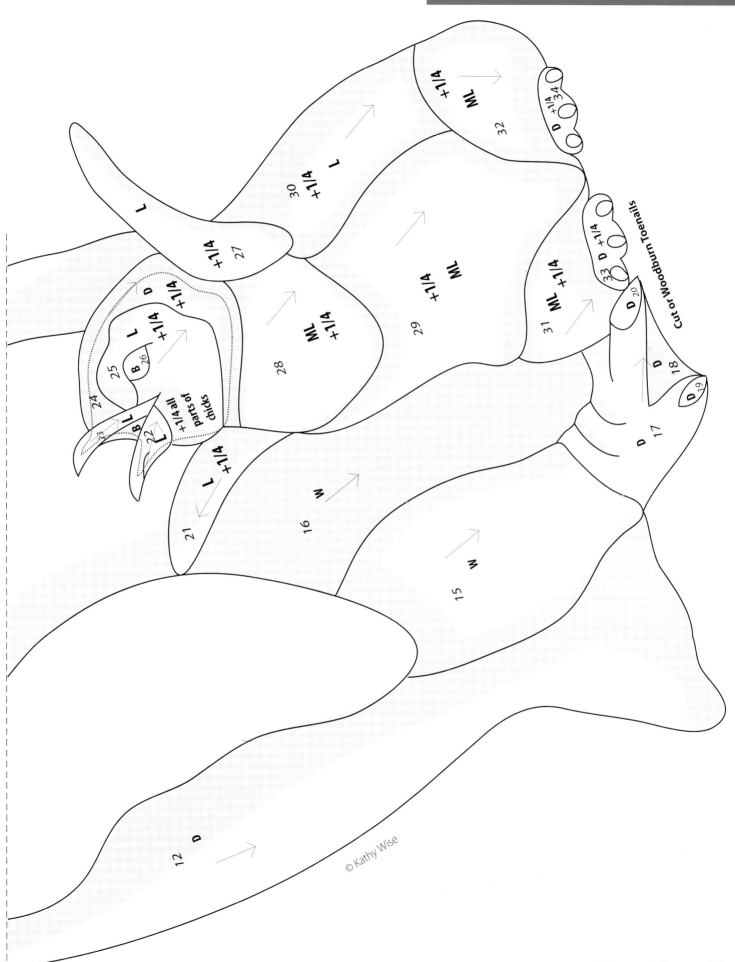

© Kathy Wise

Cut or Woodburn Toenails

+1/4 all
parts of
chicks

Fox

Wood ¾"-1" x 2" x 2" black wood such as ebony, black walnut, or your wood of choice stained or
woodburned black (eyes, nose, and mouth)

¾-1 x 4 x 5 dark wood, such as wenge, black walnut or ebony (ears)

¾ -1 x 8 x 12 white wood such as poplar, aspen or holly (ears, chin, and chest)

¾-1 x 8 x 24 red wood such as bloodwood, mahogany, cherry, or cedar (fur)

⅛-¼ x 15 x 18 lauan plywood, Baltic birch plywood, or masonite (backing board)

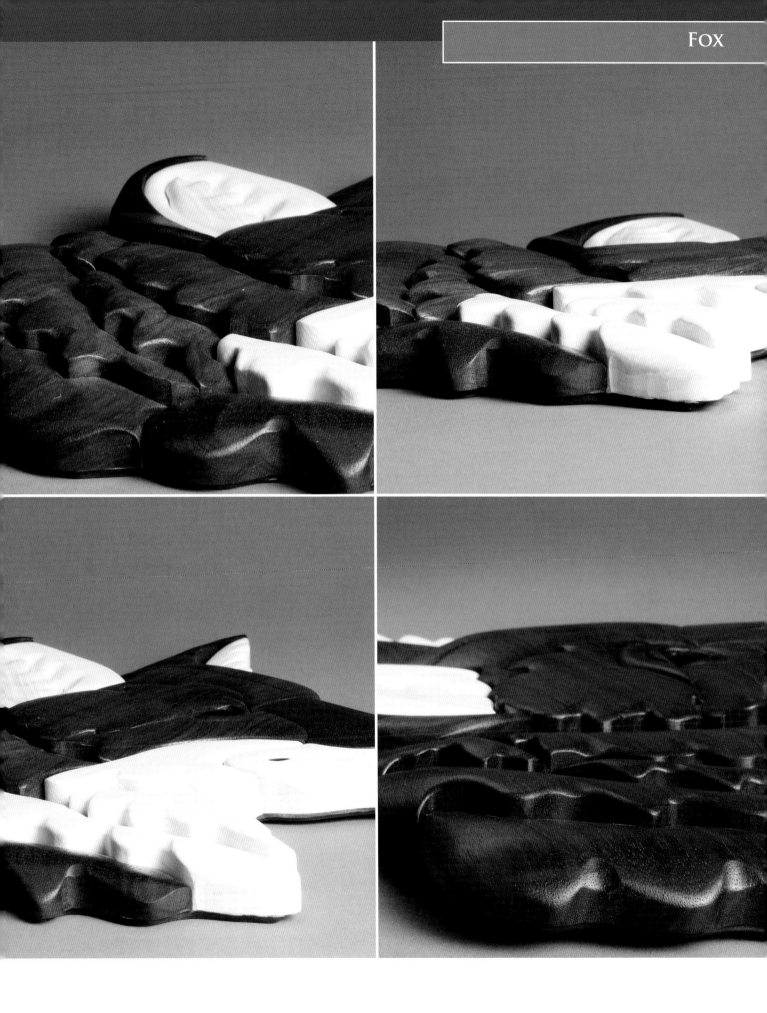

Legend

Start with ¾" wood

⟶ Grain Direction

B .... Black/Very Darkest Shade

R .... Reddish Shade of Wood

W .... Any White Wood

-¼" .... Sand or Plane Down to ¼"

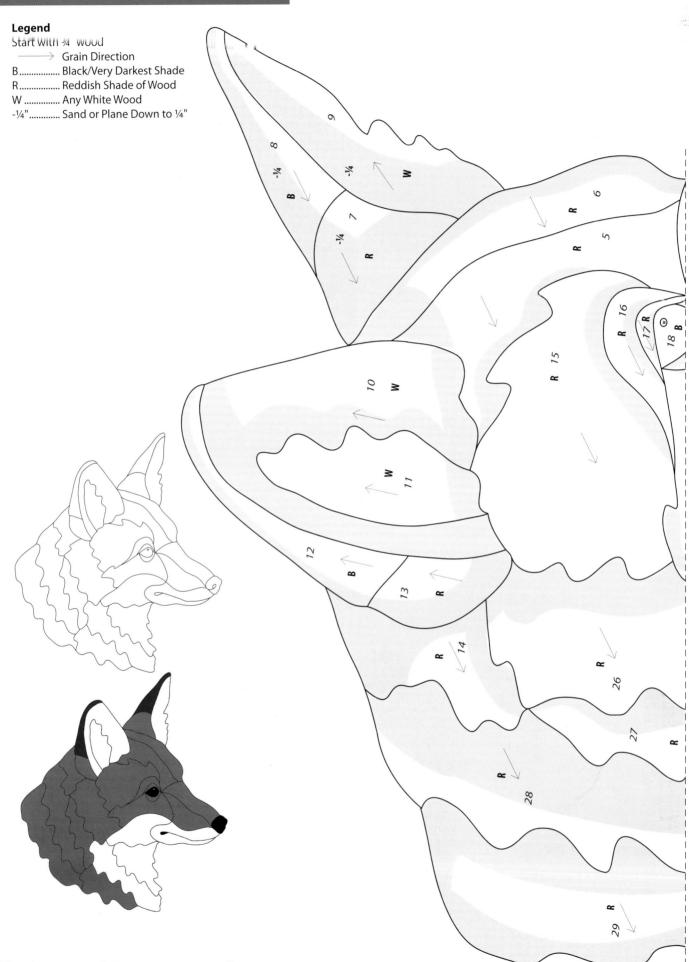

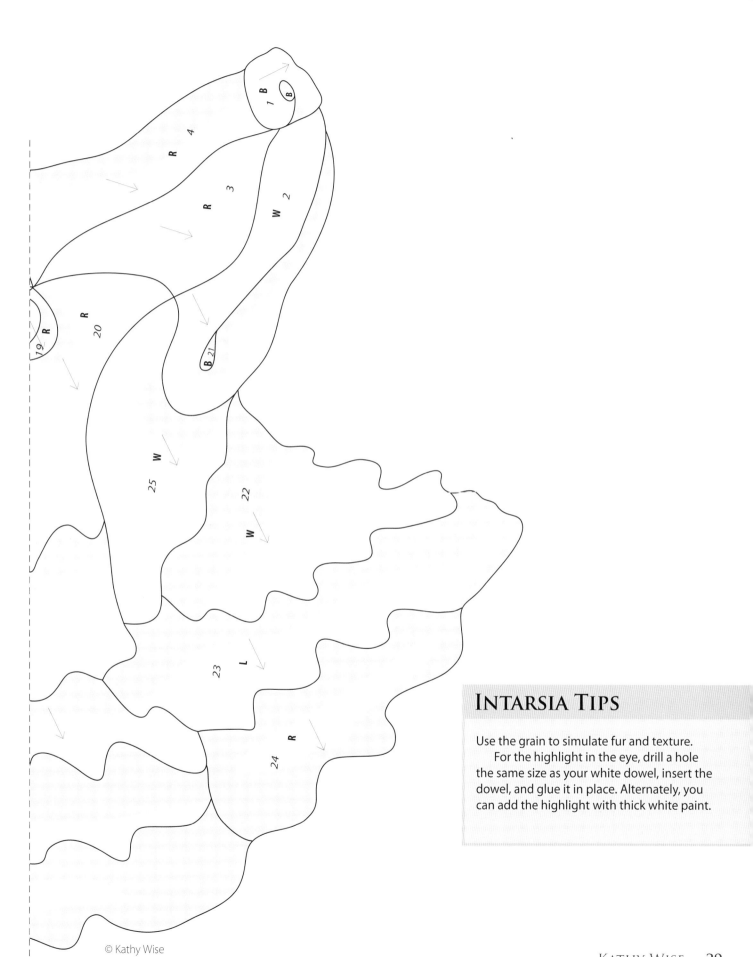

INTARSIA TIPS

Use the grain to simulate fur and texture.

For the highlight in the eye, drill a hole the same size as your white dowel, insert the dowel, and glue it in place. Alternately, you can add the highlight with thick white paint.

© Kathy Wise

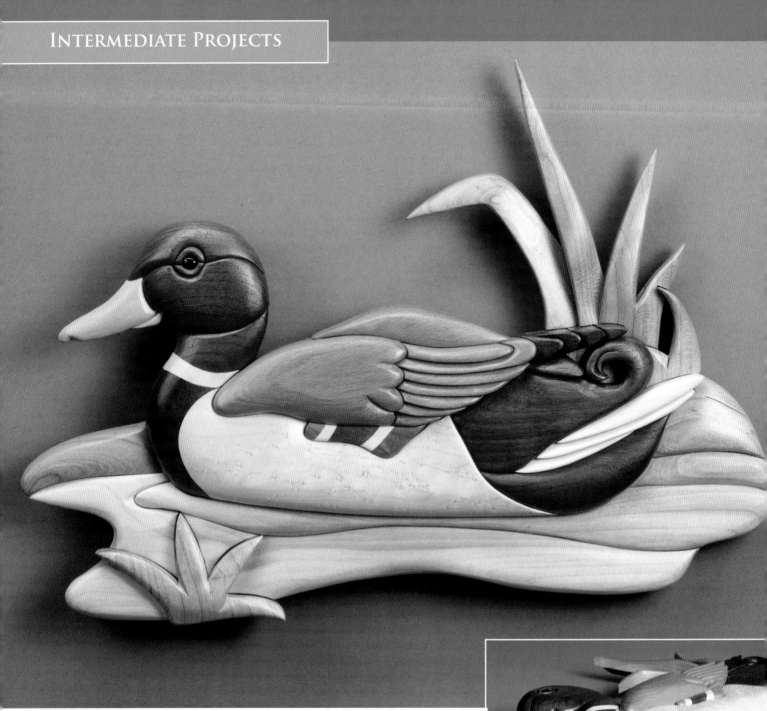

Mallard Demonstration

Wood

1" x 4" x 4" medium-dark wood such as cherry (front grass)

½" x 8" x 8" medium-dark wood such as cherry (rear grass, background)

1" x 6" x 10" medium-light wood such as bird's eye maple (body)

1" x 2" x 3" light wood such as yellowheart (beak)

1" x 5" x 8" medium wood such as beech (wing)

1" x 8" x 10" dark wood such as black walnut (head, tail, chest)

1" x 4" x 6" white wood such as poplar (neck, feathers)

½" x 4" x 18" medium-light with a dark streak, such as beech (water)

¼" x 1" x 1" black wood such as ebony, or your stained or painted wood of choice (eyes)

¼" x 12" x 14" lauan plywood or Baltic birch plywood (backing board)

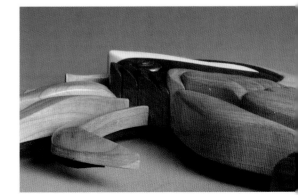

Mallard Drake

At 50 pieces, this mallard project is easy to cut and allows you to focus on details such as pattern layout, wood choice and shimming up pieces to add depth.

Remember that a pattern is simply a starting point for your finished work of art. If you want to have less pieces, eliminate some of the lines and cut areas in larger sections. You can remove some of the lines in the water area, or make the grass clump as an overlay and cut the underlying water as one piece. As you work on more intarsia projects, you will become more comfortable making design changes.

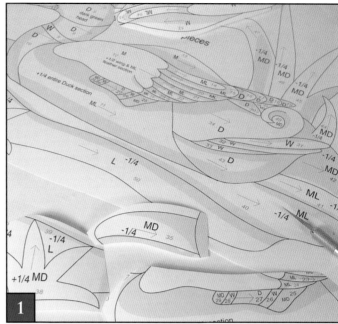

Examine the pattern. If any areas bother you or look too difficult to cut, change them. Determine where you can cut large sections of the same color with the same grain direction. You will need seven copies of the pattern. Keep one for your master copy. Cut apart each pattern piece.

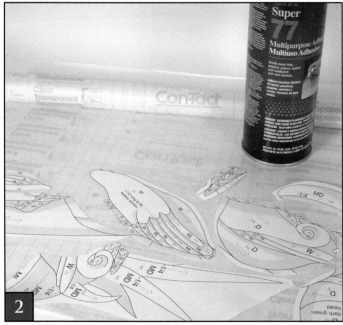

Attach the patterns to contact paper. Apply spray adhesive to the back of the pattern pieces and position the pieces on the shiny side of the contact paper. Cut apart each pattern piece and group them together according to the color and thickness of the wood.

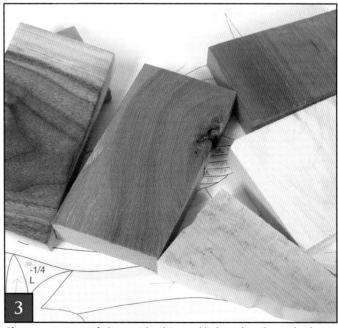

Choose your wood. Start with white and light-colored woods, then dark wood, and finally medium tones. 1"-thick stock gives you more room to add detail and texture. The dimensions listed are the bare minimum; if searching for good grain patterns, you may need twice as much. Have extra wood on hand in case you have to re-cut a piece.

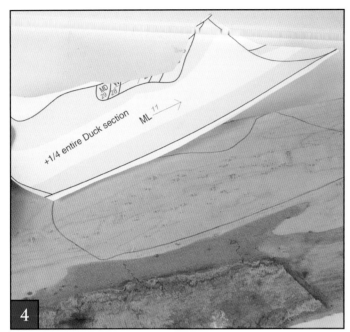

4

Choose grain patterns. I chose bird's eye maple for the body. The contrasts of light and dark in the grain produce a natural feathery effect. Be sparing with your use of wild grain; it may detract from your piece. Sometimes it helps to trace the outline of your piece onto your wood to see if the grain pattern gives the desired effect.

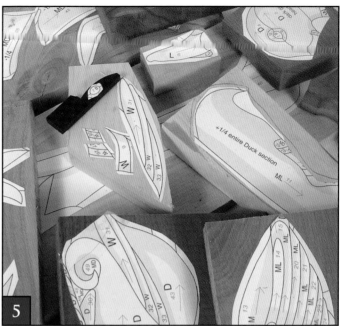

5

Peel and stick the patterns to the wood. Make sure your wood is clean, dry, and free of dust. I use yellowheart for the beak to add a spark of color. Black walnut is used for the dark areas of the bird and ebony is used for the eye. Cut the pieces down to manageable sizes on a band saw or with a large scroll saw blade, such as a #9 or #12.

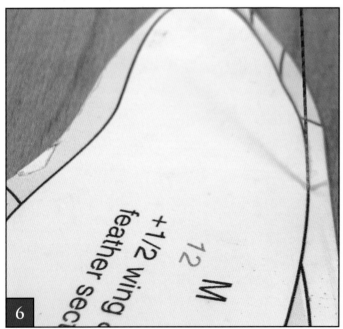

6

Cut the perimeter of the larger pieces and sections. Make sure the blade is square to the saw table. I use a #5 blade. Sand off the burr on the bottom of the wood after each cut if necessary. Keep your blade in the middle of the line. As you gain more experience, leave more of the line for a more exact fit. Number the back of each piece and place it onto a full pattern.

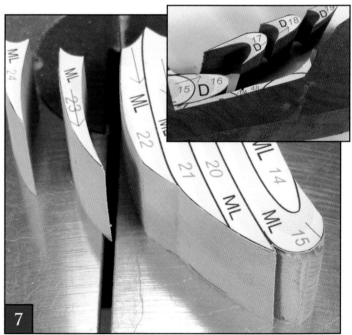

7

Cut the sections into individual pieces. Switch to a small blade, such as a #2 or #3 blade. On areas like the feathers, start with the smallest piece and move to the larger pieces. This gives you a larger piece to hold when you get to the last cut. To cut the ¼"- ½"-thick background wood, use a #5 reverse-tooth blade. Using thinner wood for these sections adds dimension and saves time when shaping.

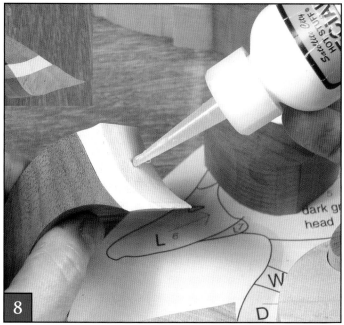

Glue the color changes together with instant glue. Make sure you have a tight fit. Glue the white band on the neck to the chest and upper neck pieces. Glue the small dark-and-white-striped feathers under the wing together. When you shape these color break areas, you want them to be connected so you have a smooth contour.

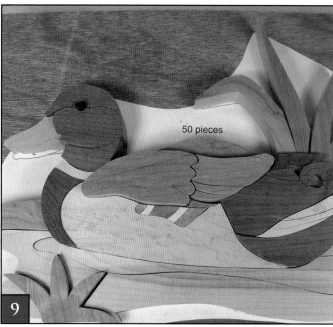

Check the pieces for fit. Place the pieces on a full-size pattern. Due to the kerf, your project will be slightly smaller than the pattern. You may need to trim some pieces to fit together better. Hold adjoining pieces up to a light source. If you see a lot of space between the pieces, you should adjust them to fit better. See sidebar on page 37.

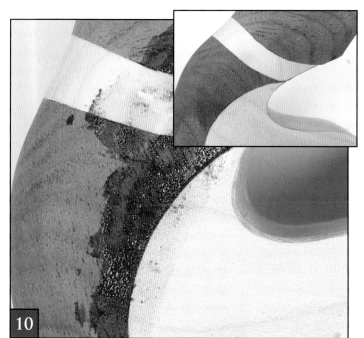

Fix gaps. For color break pieces that have a slight gap of of ¹⁄₁₆" or less, mix a small amount of sawdust with instant glue or epoxy. Use sawdust from the darkest wood surrounding the gap. Work quickly and fill in the crack, wiping most of the excess off. Sand the glue off of the top. The gap will be almost invisible after varnishing.

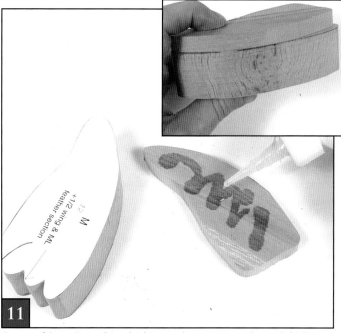

Create shims. Cut a shim thick enough to give you the 1¼" thickness you need for the wing piece from the same piece of wood. Glue it flush to the upper left area that will be exposed. Sand the two as one piece. Make a shim for under the wing feathers, but do not glue them together until after you finish sanding.

12

Start shaping the lowest areas. Use a pencil to sketch in the areas to remove, using the sanding guide on the pattern. Start with the areas that would be farthest from the viewer: the grass in the background. Replace the pieces back onto the pattern often and check the depth. Gently round the edges. Sand the grass so each piece looks like it is in front of the one next to it. Give the grass pieces a sloping curve.

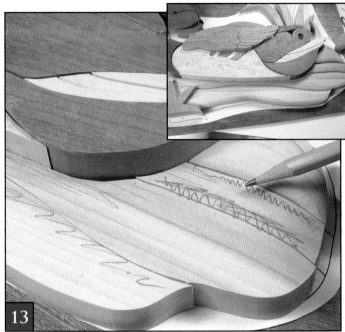

13

Continue shaping the background. Use a hobby knife to carve a small notch on piece #44 where the grass meets the ground. Mark the two small inside pieces, #48 and #49, by placing them next to the outside grass pieces to determine the correct height. Shape the water area. Mark and gently round the edges of the water up to the background piece.

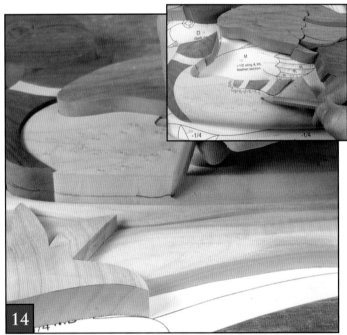

14

Shape the duck's body. Mark the bottom of your duck at the water line; you don't want to sand below this line. Round the body sections. Mark and sand any sections that need to be taken down, such as the area under a set of feathers. Mark and sand the edge of the hind end. Round and remove wood below the white feathers. Round the edges of the wing section.

15

Sand the small pieces. Use a rotary power carver or an air grinder with a ¼" or ½" sanding drum to round the areas around the duck's eye, the beak, the curled feathers on the tail, and the inside edges of the body. You can also use the small sanding drum to sand the feathers if you are not comfortable holding the small pieces against a drum sander.

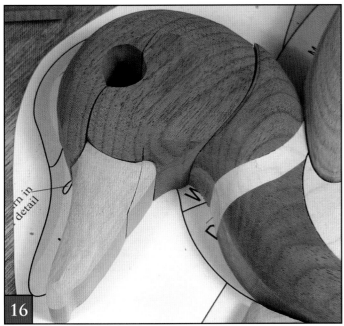

16

Sand the head. Round the edges of the head and beak. Be careful where the top of the beak meets the head. Don't remove the wood too quickly from the head or beak. It's important to get a good transition in this area.

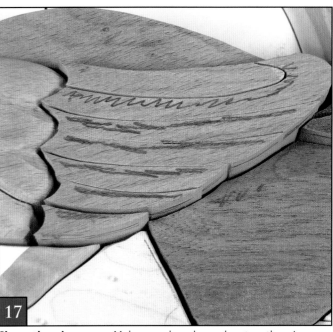

17

Shape the wing areas. Make a mark under each cut on the wing sections. Sand the feathers on a slant so the feather on top is slightly higher than the one below it. Follow the shaping guide and do not sand below your mark.

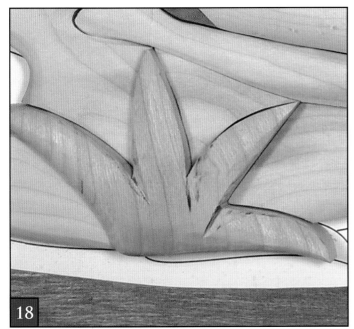

18

Shape the foreground grass area. Use a rotary power carver or an air grinder to round the edges of piece #38. The cherry burned slightly while I was shaping it, but the marks will sand off easily later.

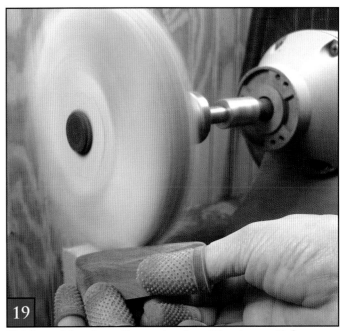

19

Finish sand the pieces. You can hand sand the pieces with fine sandpaper, but it's easier to use a 150-grit and then a 220-grit sanding mop. This step removes any scratches and leaves a polished surface.

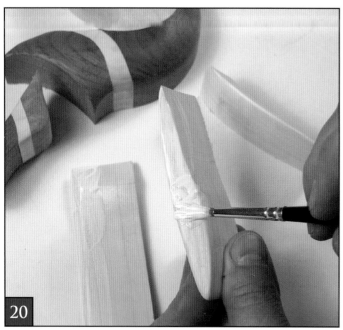

20

Apply white gel stain. To keep the poplar from yellowing, paint white gel stain onto the neck band and white feathers. Don't get the stain on the dark wood; it will show up plainly when you varnish. Carefully wipe it away from the other woods with a cotton swab.

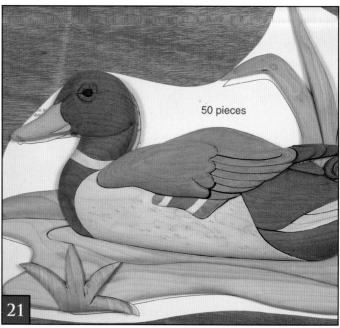

21

Make a final check of the fit and look of the project. Place it on a backing board and make sure everything looks the way you want it to. Now is the time to do any final shaping or cut replacement pieces if you are not happy with the grain or fit of any of the pieces.

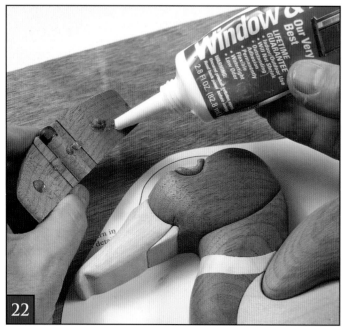

22

Tack the pieces together. Position the duck on the pattern on a flat surface. Put a few drops of 100% silicone glue or caulk between each piece, being careful to avoid any squeeze out. Let the glue dry overnight. This technique makes final gluing simple, and it allows you to space the feathers evenly to compensate for the kerf created when you cut them out of one piece.

23

Cut the backing board. Place the intarsia onto a pattern adhered to a ¼"-thick backing board. Redraw any lines on the pattern where the backing board would show. Cut inside the lines to make the backer board. Sand the surface, back, and edges. Mark the front of the board and leave that side clean and free of stain or paint. Spray paint or stain the back side a dark brown or black.

24

Attach the backing board. Spread wood glue evenly, but not too thickly, on the backing board or the intarsia. Use a few drops of instant glue and accelerator to clamp the two pieces together. Place the project onto the board and center it quickly. Press down for 30 seconds, until the instant glue sets. Place sandbags on top and allow to dry overnight. Clean up any excess glue with a wet cotton swab.

25

Apply a finish. Trim any parts of the backing board that overhang the intarsia. Touch up any exposed wood on the backing board with paint or stain. Spray several coats of varnish onto the duck. Strive to get nice, even coverage with each coat, and allow adequate drying time between coats. Read, understand, and follow the manufacturer's safety instructions on your finish of choice.

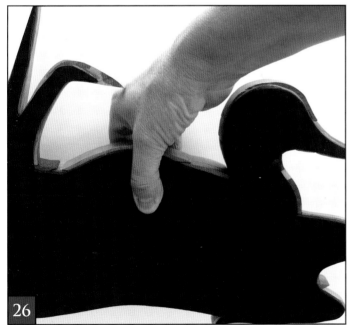

26

Attach the hanger. Hold the project between two fingers and find the correct balance point. Mark the balance point with a pencil, and drill a hole. Be careful not to drill too deep and go through to the front of your project. I suggest a mirror-style hanger.

ADJUSTING THE FIT OF THE PIECES

Re-trim the pieces that have a noticeable gap. Mark just the areas that prevent the pieces from fitting tight. Trim those areas with a new, sharp blade.

Adjust the fit of pieces with an oscillating sander. Lightly sand where the two pieces meet tightly. Sometimes you may have fed the wood into the blade too fast, which would bow the blade and give you a slight curve to the pieces. The oscillating sander goes straight up and down while turning; it's perfect for returning a square edge to your piece. Don't try to use a drum sander or belt sander; it's too hard to get a square edge.

Remember these are quick fixes, and if you have to do a lot of sanding or re-cutting, you may be better off starting over and cutting an entirely new piece. Too much adjusting will throw your entire piece off and other places that did fit previously will not fit well.

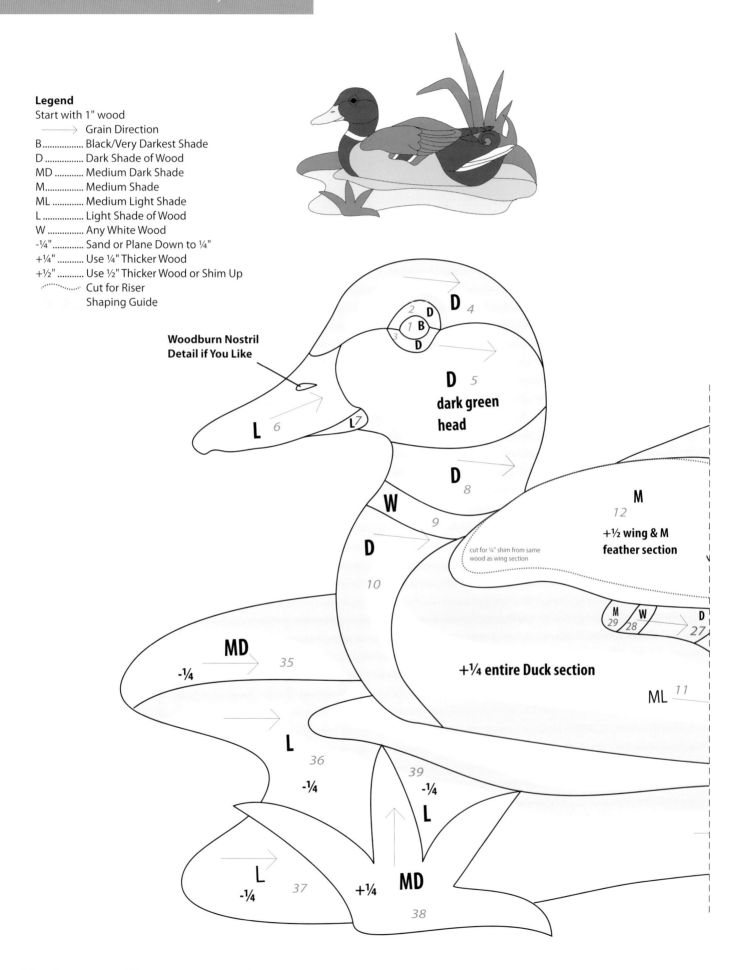

Legend

Start with 1" wood

→ Grain Direction

B .... Black/Very Darkest Shade

D .... Dark Shade of Wood

MD .... Medium Dark Shade

M .... Medium Shade

ML .... Medium Light Shade

L .... Light Shade of Wood

W .... Any White Wood

-¼" .... Sand or Plane Down to ¼"

+¼" .... Use ¼" Thicker Wood

+½" .... Use ½" Thicker Wood or Shim Up

·········· Cut for Riser

Shaping Guide

**Woodburn Nostril
Detail if You Like**

D 4

2 D

1 B

3

D

D 5

**dark green
head**

D 8

L 6

L 7

W

9

D

10

cut for ¼" shim from same
wood as wing section

M

12

**+½ wing & M
feather section**

M W D
29 28 27

MD

35

-¼

+¼ entire Duck section

ML 11

L

36

-¼

39

-¼

L

L

37

-¼

+¼

MD

38

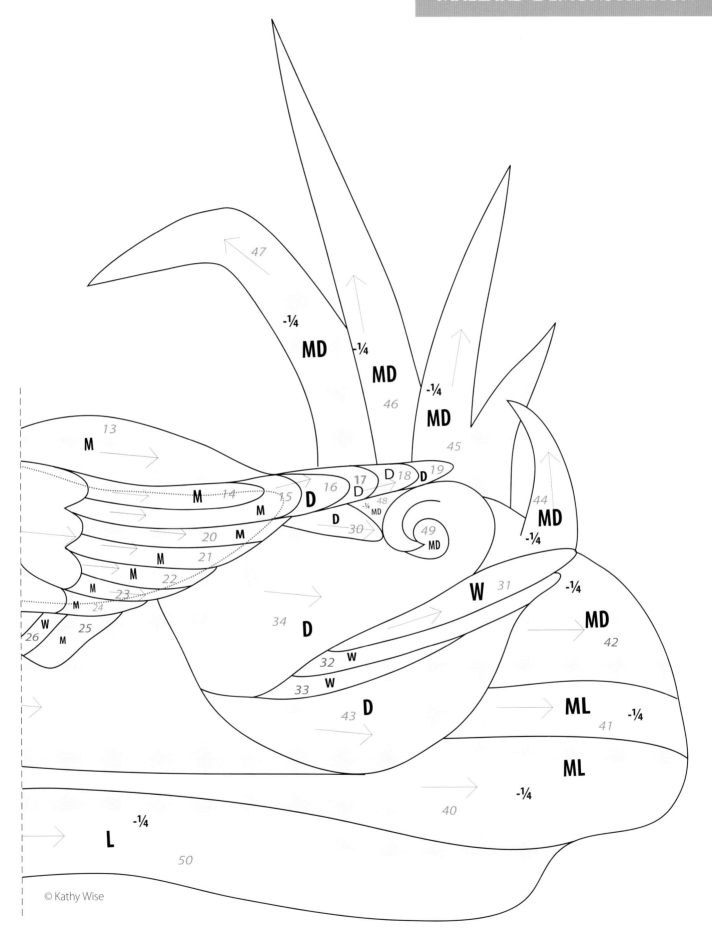

© Kathy Wise

Love Birds

Wood1" x 3" x 3" medium-dark wood such as bloodwood, cedar, or cherry

1" x 6" x 6" medium wood such as pink ivory (head)

1" x 8" x 10" light wood such as yellowheart, poplar, or cedar

1" x 5" x 5" white wood such as poplar, maple, or cedar

½" x 3" x 3" dark wood such as wenge, black walnut, or ebony

½" x 6" x 8" medium-dark wood such as black walnut, cherry, or mahogany

¼" x 1" x 1" black wood such as ebony, black walnut, or your stained/burned wood of choice

¼" x 12" x 14" masonite, lauan plywood, or Baltic birch plywood (backing board)

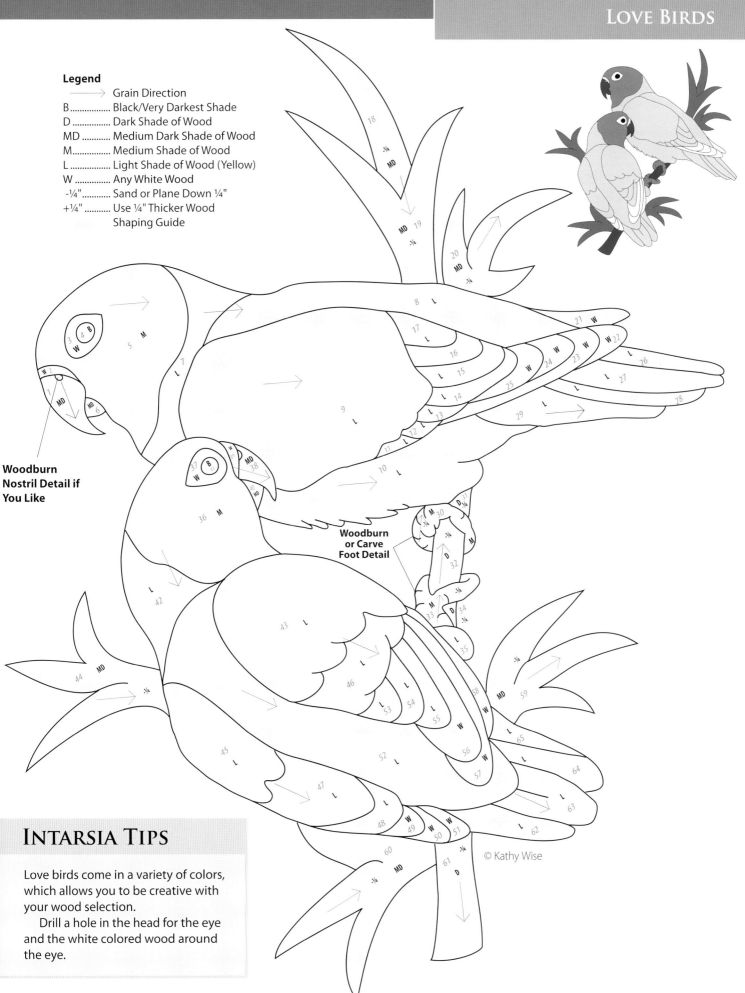

Legend

→ Grain Direction
B .... Black/Very Darkest Shade
D .... Dark Shade of Wood
MD .... Medium Dark Shade of Wood
M .... Medium Shade of Wood
L .... Light Shade of Wood (Yellow)
W .... Any White Wood
-¼" .... Sand or Plane Down ¼"
+¼" .... Use ¼" Thicker Wood
Shaping Guide

Woodburn Nostril Detail if You Like

Woodburn or Carve Foot Detail

© Kathy Wise

INTARSIA TIPS

Love birds come in a variety of colors, which allows you to be creative with your wood selection.

Drill a hole in the head for the eye and the white colored wood around the eye.

Piano Girls

Wood 1" x 10" x 27" dark wood such as black walnut (piano)
½" x 3" x 7" black wood such as ebony (piano)
1" x 6" x 3" light wood such as Australian cypress (hair)
1" x 6" x 10" medium-dark wood such as bloodwood (dress)
1" x 7" x 6" medium wood such as beech (skirt)
1" x 4" x 4" medium-light wood such as cherry (hair)
1" x 4" x 4" light wood such as birch (shirt)
¾" x 4" x 6" light wood such as poplar (keys, pages, face)
1¼" x 4" x 10" dark wood such as black walnut (bench)
¾" x 8" x 18" light wood such as curly maple (base)
¼" x 15" x 14" lauan plywood, Baltic birch plywood, or masonite (backing board)

INTARSIA TIPS

This piece relies on shaping for proper perspective. The piano starts out 1¼" thick and tapers down as it continues upward. The base of the piano starts out ¾" thick and tapers down to ¼" thick as it heads into the background. The bench is made from 1½" wood that is tapered to the back. This maintains the illusion of depth that the design depends on.

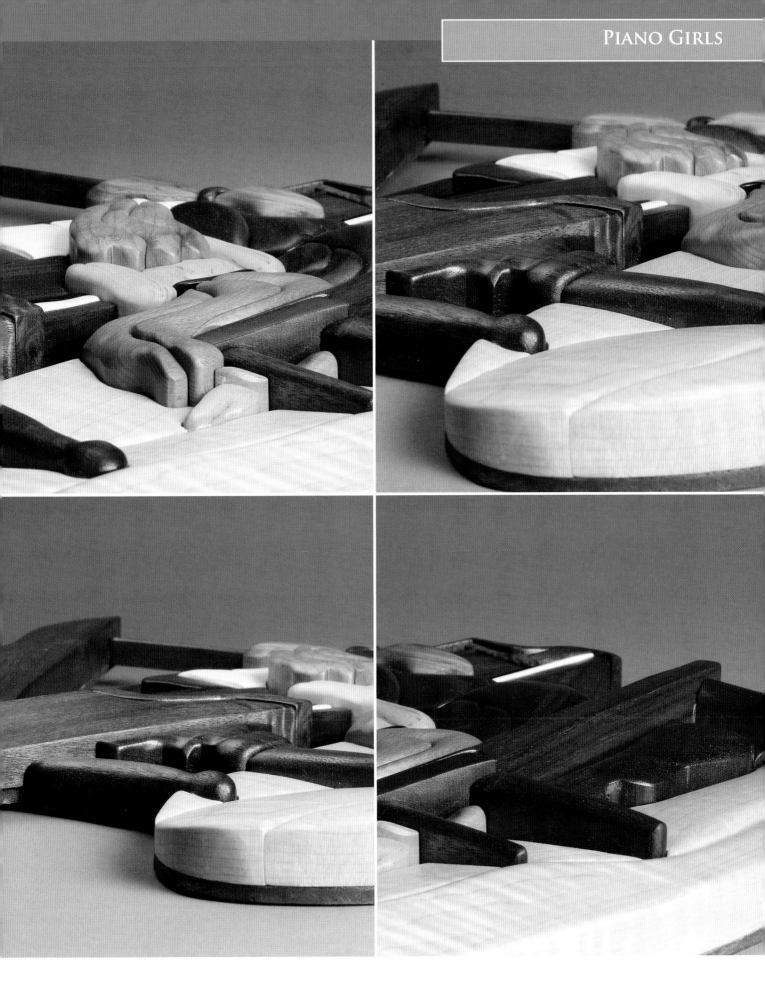

Legend

Start with 1" wood

⟶ Grain Direction

B .... Black/Very Darkest Shade of Wood

MD .... Medium Dark Shade of Wood

ML .... Medium Light Shade of Wood

M .... Medium Shade of Wood

L .... Light Shade of Wood

W .... Any White Wood

-¼" .... Sand or Plane Down ¼"

+¼" .... Use ¼" Thicker Wood

+½" .... Use ½" Thicker Wood

Shaping Guide

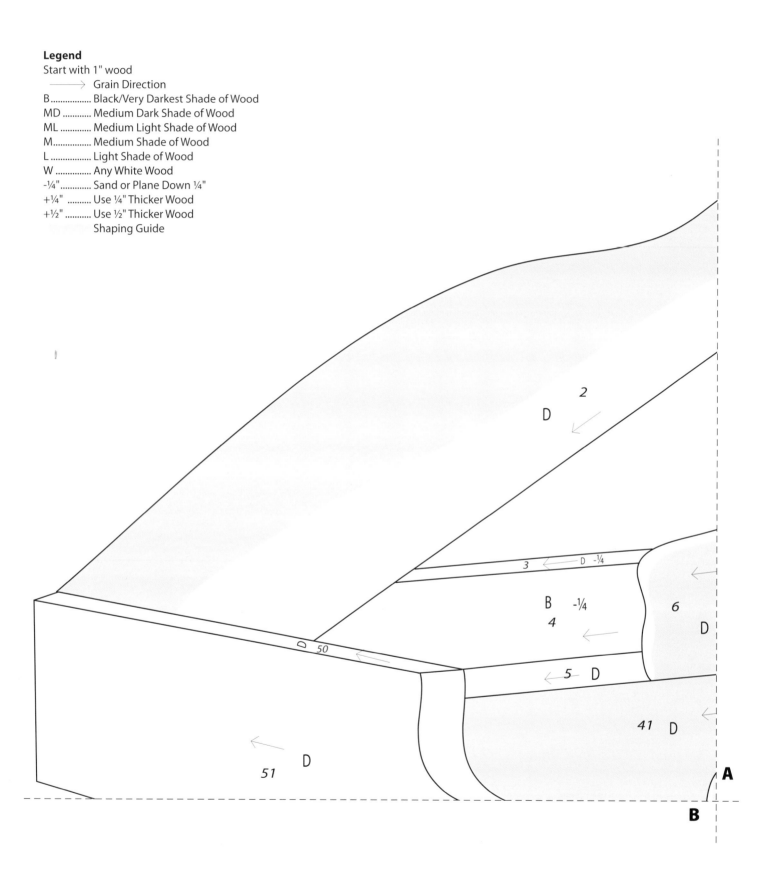

© Kathy Wise

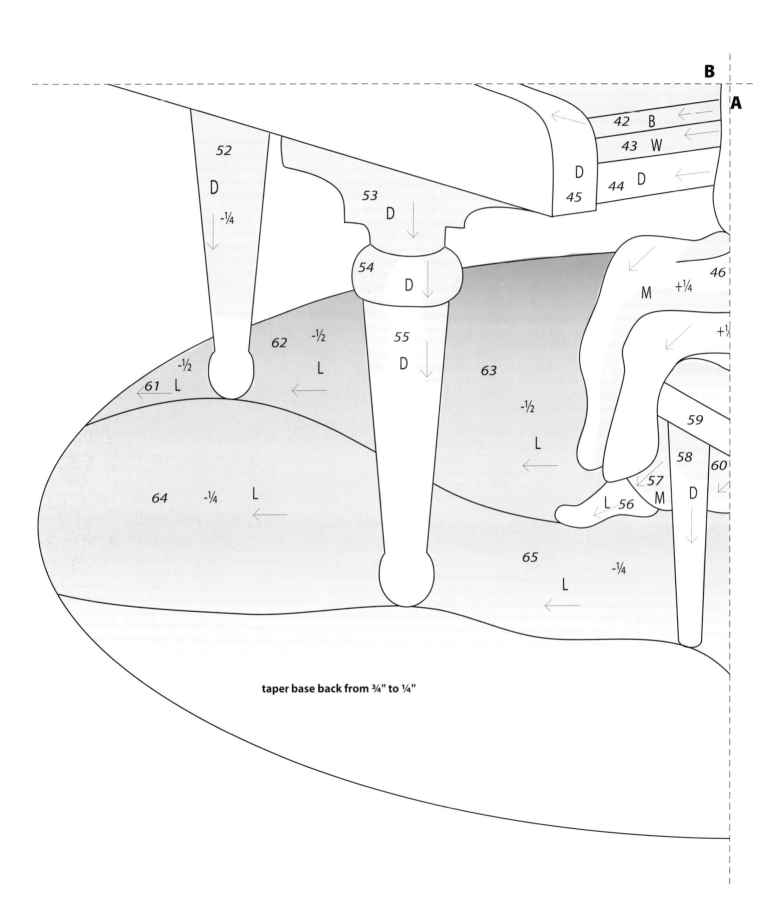

52 D -¼

53 D

54 D

55 D

42 B

43 W

44 D

45 D

46 M +¼

+¼

62 -½ L

61 L -½

63 -½ L

64 -¼ L

65 L -¼

59

58 D -¼

60

57

56 L M

taper base back from ¾" to ¼"

B A

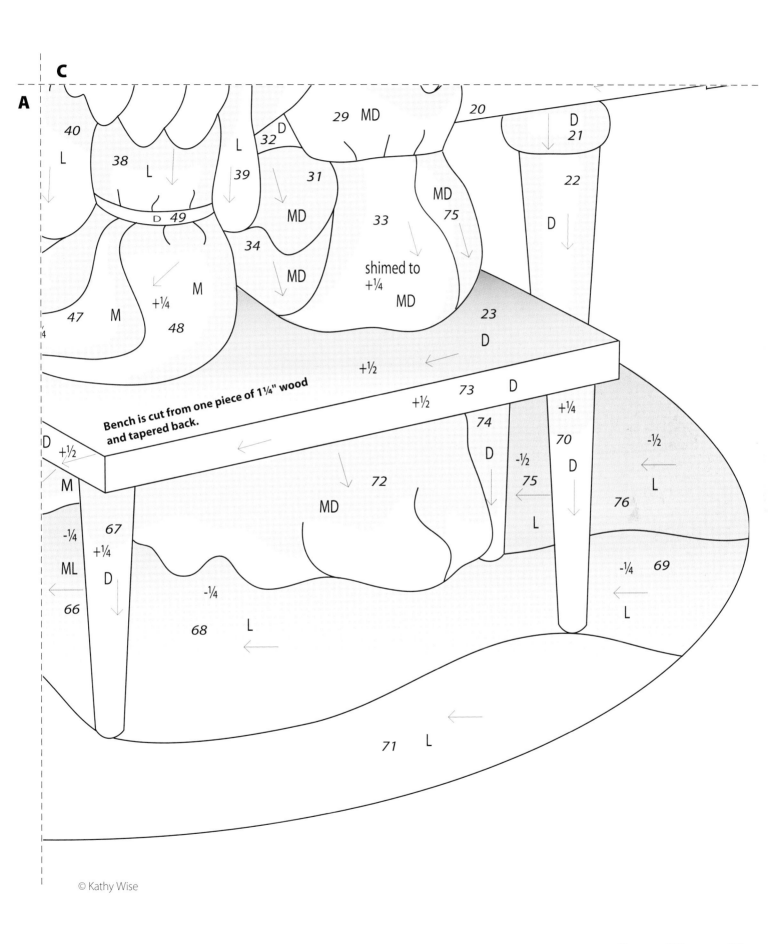

C

A

40

L

38

L

L

32 D

L

39

29 MD

20

D
21

22

31

MD

33

shimed to
+¼

MD

MD
75

D

23

D

47

M

M
+¼

48

34

MD

MD

D 49

D

+½

Bench is cut from one piece of 1¼" wood
and tapered back.

+½

73

+½

D

74

70

D
75

+¼

-½

L

76

D

+½

M

72

MD

D

L

-¼

ML

67
+¼

D

68

-¼

L

66

71

L

-¼

69

L

69

© Kathy Wise

Pool Balls

Wood

1-1¼" x 10" x 14" white wood such as ash, aspen, poplar, or maple
1" x 4" x 11" medium wood such as beech, cherry, cedar, or oak
1" x 4" x 5" dark wood such as black walnut, dark cherry, or ebony
⅛-¼" x 14" x 15" lauan plywood, Baltic birch plywood, or masonite
    painted green (backing board)

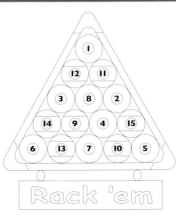

The *Pool Balls* pattern can be found
in the pattern pullout section.

INTARSIA TIPS

- Cut the balls from one piece of wood. Mark the top and bottom of the striped balls for easy reassembly. Drill blade-entry holes and cut out the centers. Then cut the striped balls into sections.

- Next, cut the replacement centers from another piece of ash. Attach the number onto the white centers. You can use a variety of pre-made numbers or paint them on. I recommend self-adhesive clock numbers. Apply a coat of varnish over the numbers to seal them in place.

- Use double-sided tape to reassemble the sections of the striped balls. Sand and shape the balls. Separate the sections and apply the colors. I used a light wash of acrylic paint that allows the wood to show through. You can also use analine dyes, since they are available in more colors than stains. Mix the dyes with alcohol to help prevent the grain from rising.

- Use small screw eyes to attach the sign to the bottom of the frame.

Lighthouse

Wood

1" x 6" x 15" medium wood such as beech (foreground)

1" x 6" x 11" medium-light wood such as light beech (foreground)

1" x 6" x 10" white wood such as poplar, aspen, or holly (lighthouse, buildings)

1" x 5" x 7" red wood such as bloodwood, cedar, or cherry (roofs, lighthouse)

1" x 9" x 15" medium-dark wood such as black walnut or wenge (bushes, frame)

½" x 2" x 2" black wood such as ebony (windows, doors)

1" x 6" x 9" dark wood such as wenge or black walnut (background)

¾" x 6" x 22" light wood such as curly maple (water)

¼" x 8" x 15" light wood such as curly maple, poplar, or ash (sky)

¼" x 5" x 15" medium-light wood such as beech (sky)

¼" x 17" x 21" masonite, lauan plywood, or Baltic birch plywood (backing board)

INTARSIA TIPS

Taper the water down to the shoreline.

Glue the red parts to the white parts so you can sand and shape the entire lighthouse as one piece.

The *Lighthouse* pattern can be found in the pattern pullout section.

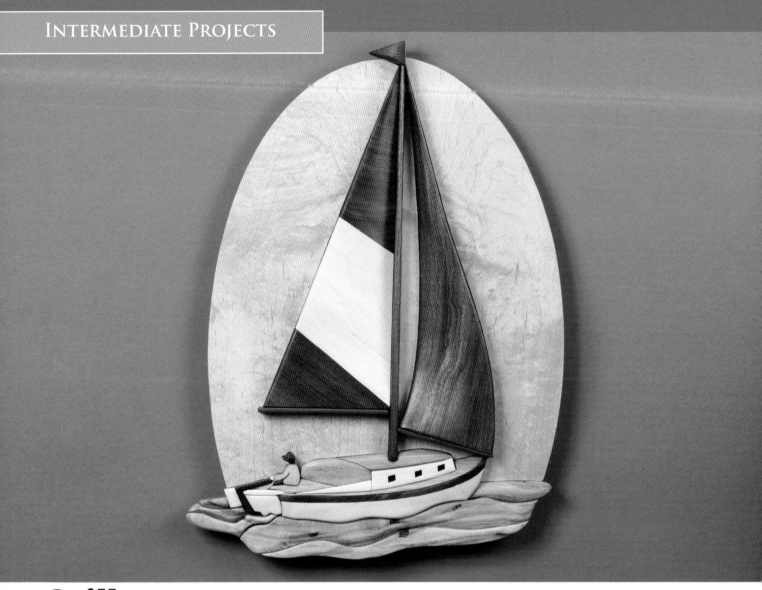

Sailboat

Wood

1" x 12" x 14" medium-light wood such as yellow pine or grey pine (boat)

1" x 8" x 18" white wood such as poplar, aspen, or holly (boat, sail)

1" x 9" x 10" dark wood such as bloodwood, cedar, or cherry (sails, boat stripe)

1" x 3" x 18" medium-dark wood such as black walnut or wenge (mast, flag)

1" x 2" x 2" medium-colored wood such as yellowheart (jacket)

1" x 3" x 3" dark wood such as wenge or black walnut (hat, rudder)

½" x 5" x 18" medium-light wood such as spalted maple (water)

¼" x 9" x 40" white-wood such as curly maple, poplar, or ash (sky)

¼" or ⅛" x 15" x 18" lauan plywood, Baltic birch plywood, or masonite (backing board)

INTARSIA TIPS

After cutting out all of the pieces, tack the two colors of the sail together with instant glue before sanding and shaping them.

Use wire to represent ropes if you want to add more detail.

The *Sailboat* pattern can be found in the pattern pullout section.

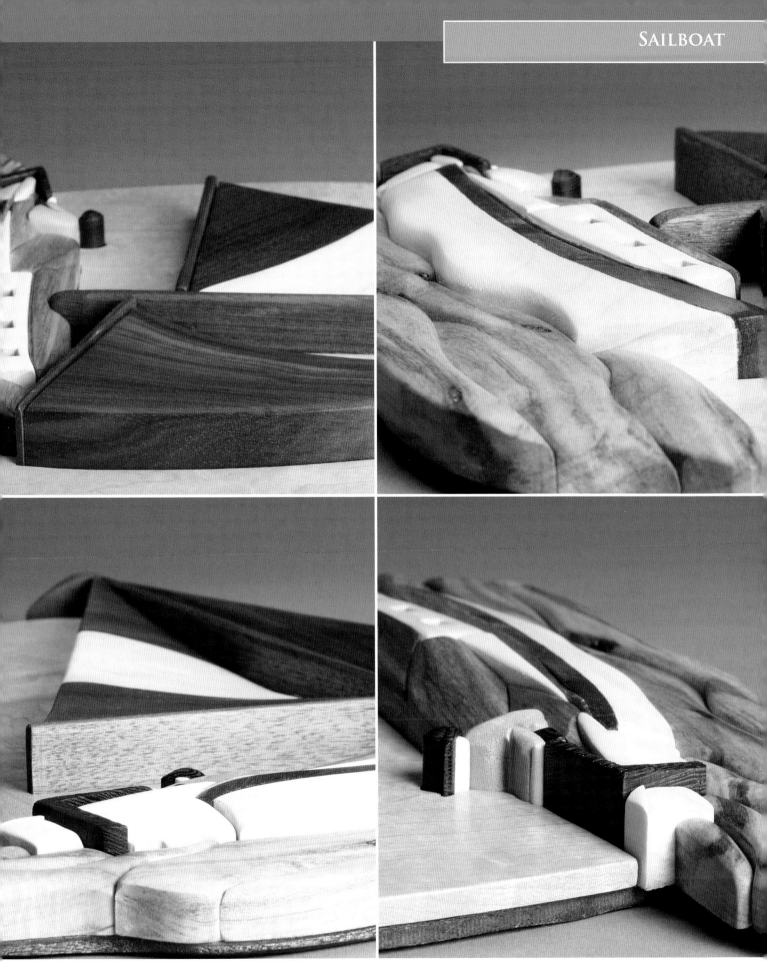

Lion Demonstration

Wood

1" x 10" x 12" medium-light wood such as sycamore (face)

1" x 8" x 13" light wood such as birch (face)

1" x 9" x 36" medium-dark wood such as beech (mane)

1" x 9" x 22" dark wood such as black walnut (mane)

¾" x 3" x 4" dark wood such as black walnut (nose)

1" x 6" x 7" white wood such as aspen (chin, muzzle)

¼" x 4" x 4" black wood such as ebony (nose, lips, eyes)

¼" x 2" x 2" yellow wood such as yellowheart (eyes)

¼" x 18" x 20" lauan plywood, Baltic birch plywood, or masonite (backing board)

½" x 15" x 18" lauan plywood, Baltic birch plywood, or masonite (risers)

The *Lion* pattern can be found in the pattern pullout section.

Lion

In this project, we will add more dimension to the project using risers and sanding techniques. We will also cover a few tips to fix mistakes and make your pieces fit together more precisely.

The flowing mane of the lion is perfect to practice contour-sanding techniques and other methods of achieving depth in an intarsia project.

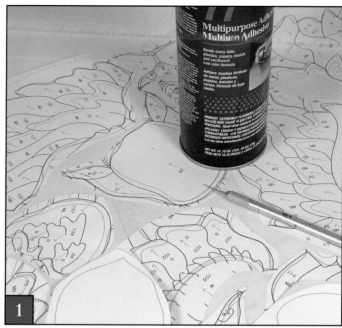

Organize your pattern pieces. You will need seven copies of the pattern. Keep a master copy. Cut apart each pattern piece. Apply spray adhesive to the back of the pattern pieces. Stick the patterns onto the shiny side of the contact paper. Cut apart each pattern piece and group them together according to color and wood thickness.

Choose the wood for the project. I use 1"-thick beech for the mane and ¾"-thick birch, ¾"-thick sycamore, and ¾"-thick aspen for the face. For the tips of the mane, I use 1"-thick black walnut. I use ebony for the pupils, nose, and lips and yellowheart for the eyes. There is so much movement expressed with the shaping of the mane that a strong grain pattern is not necessary for those sections.

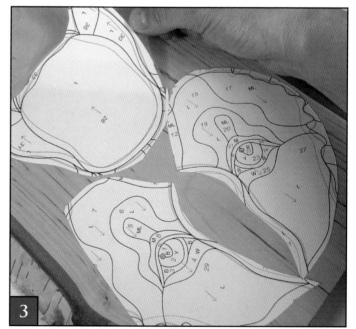

Peel and stick the patterns to the wood. Make sure your wood is clean, dry, flat, and dust-free. The birch for the lion's face has some light brown streaks that I place on the outer edges of the face and the nose section. Careful placement of your pattern pieces can make the difference between a nice intarsia project and an outstanding one. Cut the pieces into more manageable sections.

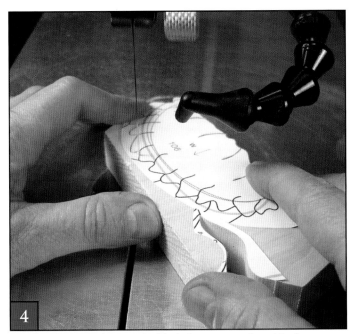

Cut the pieces. Make sure the blade is square to the table. As you cut, keep your blade right in the middle of the line. Cut slowly and carefully on lines that meet other color sections; the better your cuts, the better your fit will be. For a tighter fit, cut slightly to the outside of the line and leave about half of the line.

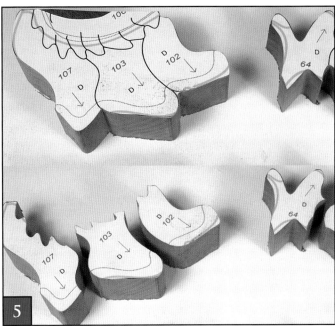

Number the bottom of each piece. With so many similar pieces, it's easy to lose track of which piece fits where. Save yourself time trying to reassemble the pieces later by marking the bottom of each piece as you cut it. Use a pencil, because ink or marker can bleed when you varnish and be hard to remove.

Check the pieces for fit. Position the cut pieces on a full-size pattern attached to a backing board. Place the lion on the floor and take a step back to look at it. This will give you a better idea of how the lights and darks are working in the piece. If you do not like the color or grain direction of a piece, cut a new one.

Adjust the fit of pieces. You want all the pieces to fit tightly together. Lightly sand any trouble areas with an oscillating sander. Mark the tight spots with a pencil and sand off a little at a time. If you are having trouble getting the pieces to fit with minor sanding, it's best to cut a new piece.

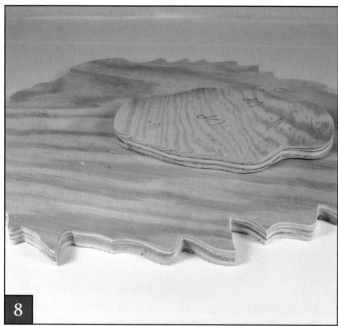

8

Cut the risers. Risers are inexpensive wood used to raise up specific sections. Use a ½"-thick riser under the inside mane and head area and another ½"-thick riser under the nose and chin area. Risers should be put in place before any sanding starts. Make sure your risers are flat and sanded clean. Mark the top.

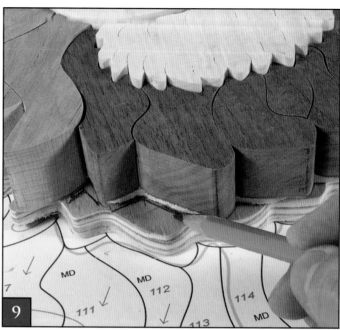

9

Trim the risers to fit. Make sure none of the riser sticks out farther than the cut pieces or it will interfere with the fit of the pieces. Place the cut pieces onto the riser and mark any parts of the riser that overhang the pieces. The riser can be slightly undersized. Trim the riser with the scroll saw.

10

Assemble the mane. Use cyanoacrylate (CA) glue to join color breaks. Shape these sections as one piece so you can sand it to a smooth contour. Check your seams. If you have any small gaps, you can fill them with CA glue mixed with sawdust, as demonstrated in the Mallard Drake tutorial (page 33). Glue the sections of muzzle together using CA glue. Sand the back of all the pieces flat.

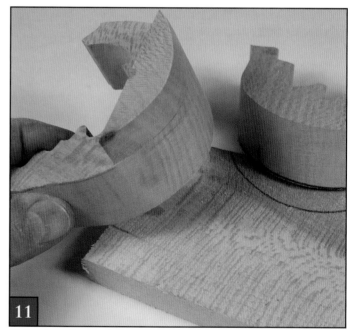

11

Make risers for the ears. Cut the ears from 1¼"-thick stock, or cut them from ¾"-thick wood and add a ½"-thick riser of the same wood to the bottom. Glue the riser flush to the top edge of the ear that is exposed and sand it smooth. Trim back the riser beneath the face if it interferes with the ear. Alternately, cut the dotted lines on the pattern to add extra tufts of hair and use a regular plywood riser.

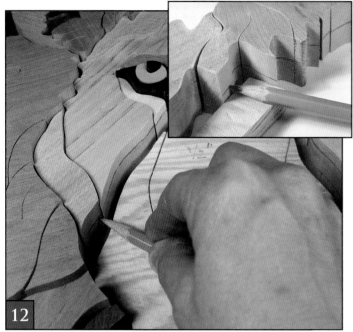

12

Mark the inside levels. Position a piece of the scrap riser stock next to the inside edge of the outer mane pieces. Make a line ⅛" higher than the riser. Remove the inside muzzle section from the riser and make a mark about ⅛" higher along the entire inside of the face pieces. Do not sand below this line.

13

Mark the areas to sand down on the mane. Use a pencil to shade the sections on each piece that need shaping. Refer to the sanding guide on the pattern. These areas will give separation to the individual tufts of the mane and add depth, dimension, and texture to your finished intarsia.

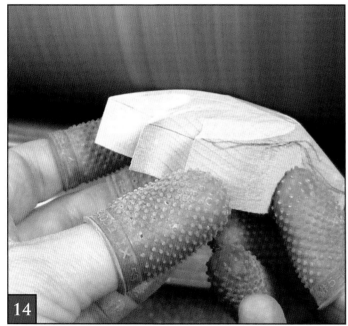

14

Shape the pieces. Start with the outside of the mane. Sand down to your line with a large drum sander. Push your piece into the drum and then back off in a buffing motion. The more pressure you apply, the more wood is removed. Make sure your sander is not over-inflated; it will not give enough when you push into it. Once the piece has the basic shape, switch to the smaller drum with fine sandpaper.

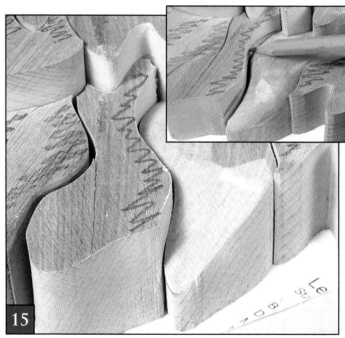

15

Work your way around the mane. Use the smaller drum to round the surface more. You may have to sand against the grain in order to get the pieces shaped. Roll the pieces to get a nice slope and then sand in the direction of the grain to remove scratches. Use the piece you just sanded to mark the piece next to it. Sand, mark, and sand again. Replace the piece back to the pattern often to check your levels.

Mark the height of the inside of the mane. Use the outer mane pieces you just shaped as a guide. You want the inner mane section to be higher than the outer section. The different layers add depth and volume to the mane. Continue sanding pieces until you have the mane sanded and shaped.

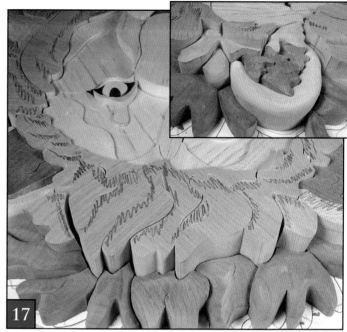

Shape the ear sections. Mark the ears, using the sanding guide on the pattern. Round the edges of the ears and taper them toward the head. Use a 2" drum sander to get a slope towards the inside of the ear. The dark hair inside the ear should stick above the ear. Sand the hair next to the ear, but make sure it is higher than the ear itself.

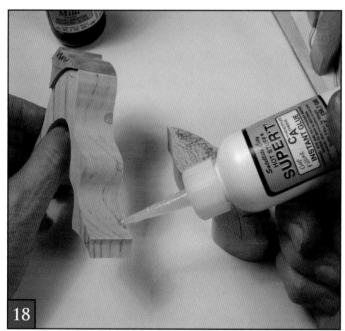

Spot glue pieces for sanding. Use one or two drops of thick CA glue near the bottom of each piece to hold the face sections together. Add a quick spray of accelerator and press the two pieces together. Press the pieces down on a flat surface and rotate as the glue sets. Make sure the two pieces are completely flat and fit tightly. Shape the pieces as one for better contour. Be careful when separating small, delicate parts. If two pieces are stubborn and don't break with a quick rap on a hard surface, cut along the joint with the scroll saw.

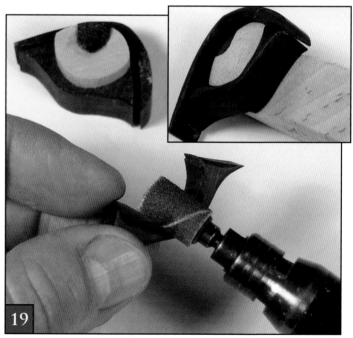

Shape and assemble the eye. Glue the ebony pupil into the yellowheart iris. Round the eye section with a rotary tool or air grinder. Make sure the black areas fit tightly. Add the white highlight to each eye by drilling a small hole and gluing in a stick of white wood. Sand the white wood flush with the eye. Buff the eye on the sanding mop and glue all of the sections together. Note: The upper and lower eyelids should be slightly higher than the eye.

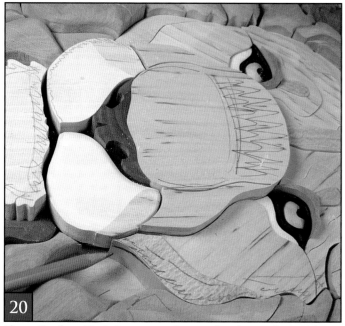

20

Shape the face. Mark the areas to shape, using the sanding guide on the pattern. Pay special attention to the area that meets the muzzle; be sure not to sand below the line and expose the riser. Start rounding the outside edge of the face.

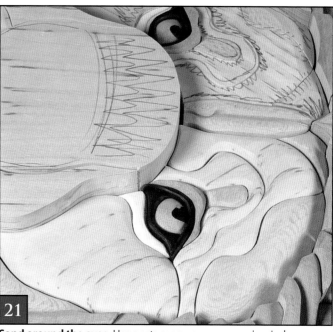

21

Sand around the eyes. Use a rotary power carver or air grinder equipped with a ¼"-½"-diameter, 120-grit sanding drum. Replace the pieces often to check for fit. Don't worry about the mane section closest to the face yet.

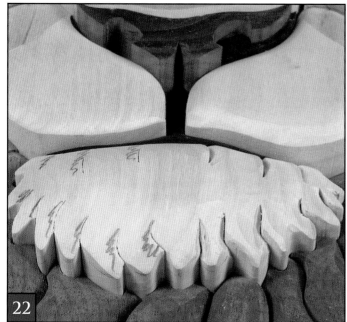

22

Shape the muzzle and chin. Round the chin and the two muzzle pieces, using the sanding guide on the pattern. Shim-up the ebony lip piece to the correct height. Use a ½"-diameter sanding drum to shape the small hair cuts around the top and bottom edges. A carving knife works well to clean out the cuts and the sanding mop will smooth away the rough edges later. I use the sanding drum to put little "dimples" between each cut line to give the chin a fluffy, hairy look.

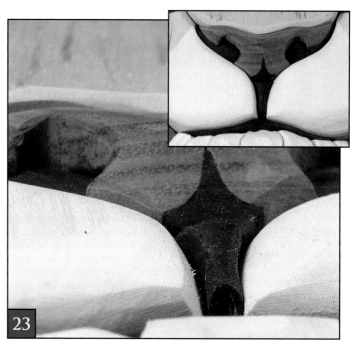

23

Shape the nose section. Add a ⅛"-thick riser to the nose section to provide more room to sand and shape the area. Round the nose and top of the nose. Mark the areas to remove and taper piece #28, which is above the nose, down to meet the face sections. Taper the side pieces (#30 and #31) down to the face section. Add the nostril holes with the ½"-diameter sanding drum. Sand the black nostrils and the black pieces between the muzzle pieces and glue them in place.

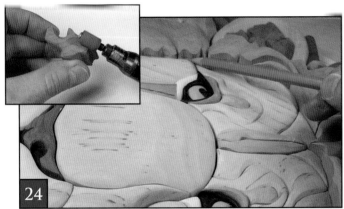

24

Shape the mane area next to the face. Mark the level of the face around the inside of the mane section and taper the wood down to that level. Adjust the depth of the entire mane wherever you can. Do not expose the risers. Use the ¼" sanding drum to sand the small curves and add extra contouring. Assemble all the pieces and make any changes or fitting corrections now.

25

Finish sand the pieces. You can hand sand with fine sandpaper, but I prefer to use a 150-grit and then a 220-grit sanding mop to speed up the process. Hold small pieces with needle-nose pliers. If you find any gaps where two colors meet, fill them with epoxy or CA glue mixed with sawdust. See the Mallard Drake tutorial on page 33 for more information on this technique.

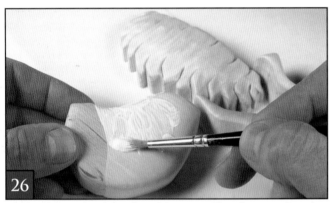

26

Apply white gel stain to the white areas. The white wood tends to yellow with age after varnish is applied. To keep the wood looking white, apply two coats of white gel stain, according to the manufacturer's instructions, and allow the pieces to dry overnight. Don't get the white gel stain on the other wood. Use a cotton swab to clean up any unwanted stain.

27

Apply a satin gel varnish to the face. Tack the face together with CA glue, and glue it to the risers with wood glue. Apply varnish to the face, and wipe as much off as possible. Blow extra varnish out of the cracks with an air compressor and wipe up the extra varnish. Use cotton swabs to reach tight areas. Apply two coats according to the manufacturer's instructions and allow to dry overnight.

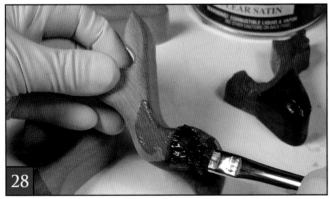

28

Apply the satin gel varnish to the mane. Apply two coats of gel varnish to each piece. Cover the sides and tops with a brush. Let the varnish dry overnight. Apply a gloss varnish to the eyes for a lifelike shine.

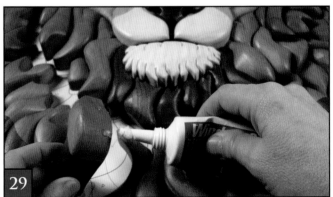

29

Tack mane sections together with 100% silicone glue. Position the mane pieces on a pattern on a flat surface. Divide the mane into eight smaller sections. Put a few drops of silicone glue between each piece. Replace each section as you tack them together. Allow the silicone to dry overnight.

Cut the backing board. Place the assembled intarsia onto a pattern adhered to a ¼"-thick backing board. Redraw lines on the pattern where it shows through. Cut ⅛" inside the lines. Sand the front, back, and edges. Mark the front side of the board and keep it free of stain or paint. Paint or stain the backside with a dark brown or black for a finished look.

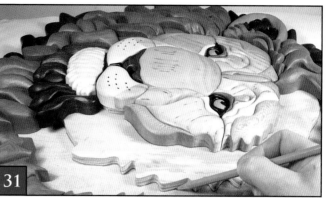

Glue the face section and risers to the backing board. Position all the sections on the backing board and remove sections as necessary to access the risers. Mark around the risers so you know where to position them. Glue the face and risers onto the backing board with wood glue. Use CA glue to "clamp" the two pieces together while the wood glue is setting.

Glue the mane to the backing board. Use your glue of choice. I use two-part, five-minute epoxy, because it sets quickly and is permanent. Start with the mane sections closest to the face. As you glue them in place, push the outer sections of the mane up against the inside sections to make sure they are in the correct position. Let the epoxy set; then move on to the next section until all the pieces are glued in place.

Attach the hanger to the back. Trim any overhanging backing board. Touch up any exposed areas on the backing board with stain or paint. On large, heavy pieces, I use two screw eyes and picture wire. Mark the location for the screw eyes, and drill pilot holes. Thread the screws into the holes, thread the wire through the screw eyes, and twist the wire ends tightly around the wire and screw eyes.

INTARSIA TIPS

Adjusting for fit: Hold the two problem pieces together as tightly as you can and re-cut along the line. This takes a bit of practice, so experiment on scrap wood first. You can also put a drop or two of CA glue on the pieces or tape them together, but pressing them together works best for me. You may have to re-cut the line two or more times depending on how large the gap is. The pieces will draw closer each time you cut. Be sure to have adequate ventilation because the blade heats up when cutting, and if it burns the CA glue, toxic fumes will be released. If you have to do a lot of sanding or re-cutting on a single piece, you may be better off cutting an entirely new piece. Too much adjusting will throw your whole project off, and other places that did fit in the beginning may end up not fitting later.

Rattlesnake

Wood

1" x 8" x 27" medium-dark wood such as black walnut

1" x 8" x 27" medium wood such as oak

1" x 2" x 9" medium-light wood such as beech (under belly spots)

1" x 8" x 27" light wood such as poplar

1" x 3" x 3" black wood such as wenge or ebony (tail)

1¼" x 4" x 5" medium wood such as cherry (rattle)

½" x 1" x 2" black wood such as ebony (eyes)

¼" x 16" x 18" lauan plywood, Baltic birch plywood, or masonite (backing board)

INTARSIA TIPS

Both a beginner and advanced version of this pattern are provided on the pattern pullout section, allowing you to choose the complexity.

Cut the rattle from 1¼"-thick wood and taper it on the front and back to make it stand out. Sand a slight bevel onto each ring of the rattle.

For a more realistic look, add the optional tongue from light wood or leather.

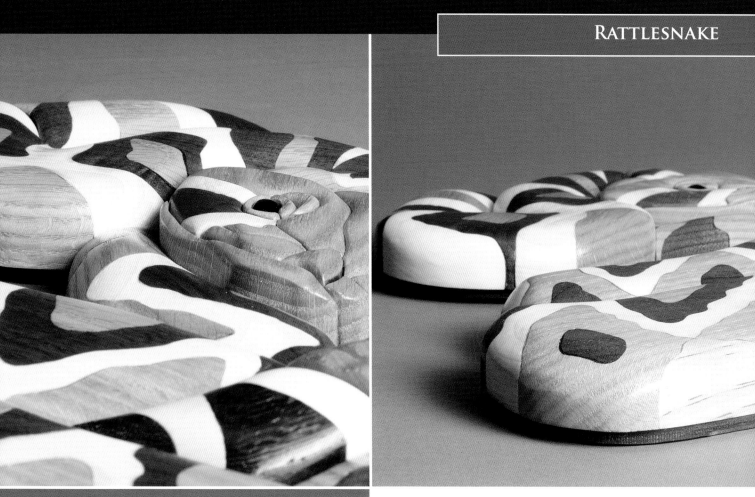

The *Rattlesnake* pattern can be found in the pattern pullout section.

Barn Scene

Wood

1" x 7" x 12" medium wood such as cherry (fence)
1" x 8" x 10" dark wood such as black walnut (cow)
¾" x 9" x 12" white wood such as poplar (barn)
¾" x 10" x 12" medium-dark wood such as black walnut (barn)
¾" x 3" x 12" medium-light wood such as yellow pine (Mail Pouch letters)
¾" x 7" x 20" light wood such as a light shade of beech (ground)
¾" x 7" x 20" medium-light wood such as beech (ground)
½" x 5" x 8" dark wood such as wenge (trees)
½" x 4" x 4" light wood such as ash (buildings)
¾" x 8" x 16" medium wood such as cedar (roofs)
¼" x 7" x 24" light wood such as curly maple (sky)
¾" x 2" x 4" black wood such as ebony (eyes, windows)
1" x 2" x 110" medium wood such as beech (frame)
½" x 21" x 26" masonite, lauan plywood, or Baltic birch plywood (backing board)

INTARSIA TIPS

The frame is cut from 2"-thick wood; you can add a 45° miter to each corner, or use the medium-dark wood to make the contrasting corners as shown in the pattern.

Since the sky is only ¼" thick, the frame and thick pieces give the project a shadow-box effect. Many of the pieces use ½"-thick risers, as indicated on the pattern, to give the project depth without breaking the bank.

The *Barn Scene* pattern can be found in the pattern pullout section.

Calf Roper

Wood

1¼" x 8" x 24" dark wood such as black walnut (calf)

1" x 8" x 12" dark wood such as black walnut or wenge (mane, tail)

1" x 6" x 6" medium wood such as beech or cedar (pants, stirrups)

1" x 9" x 5" black wood such as ebony, wenge, or black walnut (eyes, hoofs, boots)

¾" x 8" x 8" dark wood such as black walnut (vest)

¾" x 4" x 4" white wood such as poplar, ash, or maple (face, blaze)

1" x 6" x 7" medium-dark wood such as wenge (hat, glove, vest)

1" x 9" x 24" cherry (horse)

1¼" x 6" x 8" cherry (horse neck/head)

¼" x 19" x 6" medium-tone wood such as hickory or cedar (ground strip)

⅝" x 12½" x 58" light wood such as ash (background, rope)

1½" x 9" x 4" light and medium light wood such as sycamore (chaps)

1" x 6" x 9" red wood such as bloodwood (shirt)

1" x 6" x 18" medium wood such as cedar (saddle/bridle)

1" x 1" x 1" yellow wood such as yellowheart (belt buckle)

¼" or ⅛" x 18" x 15" lauan plywood, Baltic birch plywood, or masonite (backing board)

8' of rope molding (trim, optional)

The *Calf Roper* pattern can be found in the pattern pullout section.

INTARSIA TIPS

Trim the edges of the backing board with rope molding stained to the desired color. Cut each rope piece section apart and sand it slightly concave before gluing it to the outside edge.

Use shims to add height to parts of the chaps and saddle.

Use overlays for the rope, calf tail, and rein. Embellish the saddle, chaps, mane, and tail with a woodburner.

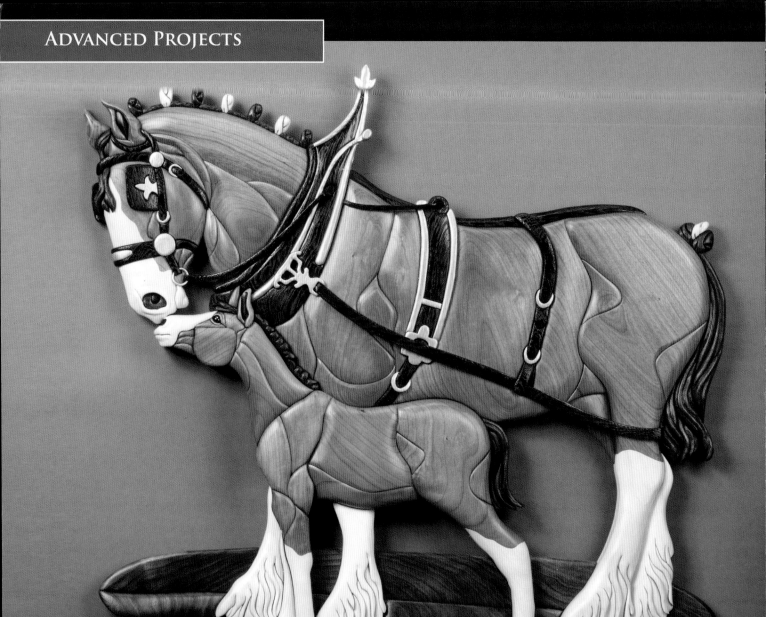

Clydesdale & Colt

Wood

1" x 5" x 10" dark wood such as black walnut (tails, manes)
1" x 10" x 48" medium wood such as cherry (horse body)
1¼" x 6" x 7" white wood such as poplar (colt's feet and face)
1¼" x 8" x 14" medium wood such as cherry (colt's body)
1" x 8" x 15" white wood such as poplar (horse's feet and nose)
1" x 4" x 4" black wood such as ebony (hooves, eyes, and noses)
¾" x 2" x 5" red wood such as bloodwood (ribbons)
¾" x 8" x 24" black wood such as wenge (harness)
¾" x 8" x 25" dark wood such as black walnut (base)
¼" x 22" x 22" masonite, lauan plywood or Baltic birch plywood
      (backing board)

INTARSIA TIPS

Cut all of the pieces marked "S" (for silver) from the same piece you cut the harness from. Then paint the pieces silver.

For several parts of the harness and reins, I cut and shaped overlays and glued them on top of the solid backing; you can also cut and shape each piece separately.

I use a piece of aluminum wire for the bit, but you can also cut it from wood and paint it.

In addition to using a gloss varnish on the eyes, I applied the gloss varnish to the shiny harness.

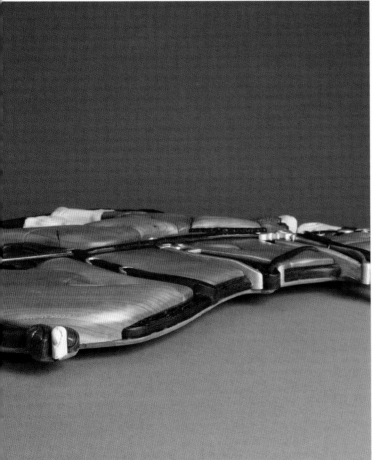

The *Clydesdale & Colt* pattern can be found in the pattern pullout section.

Eagle

Wood

1" x 10" x 27" dark wood such as black walnut (wing and body)

½" x 5" x 7" dark wood such as black walnut (wing)

¾" x 8" x 12" dark wood such as black walnut (wing)

1" x 8" x 8" white wood such as poplar (head and tail)

1" x 6" x 6" light wood such as white pine (head and tail)

1" x 4" x 5" yellow wood such as yellowheart (feet and beak)

¼" x 10" x 21" medium-colored wood such as bird's eye maple (cloud)

¼" x 22" x 30" plywood for backing board

INTARSIA TIPS

Some of the smaller pieces do not have numbers; mark them with the closest number.

Follow the grain direction arrow for each wing section. The wing sections are cut from one piece of wood, so they are easier to cut than they look, but they do require the use of a smaller blade, such as a #2 or #3.

When shaping the individual feathers, take wood off the same side and edge in each group of feathers.

The *Eagle* pattern can be found in the pattern pullout section.

KATHY WISE

Kathy Wise poses with *Whitetail Woods* (1,100 pieces, 4½' x 5').

Although Kathy Wise was a city girl for most of her childhood, she has always had a strong love for animals. When she was a teenager, her family moved to a rural area in Michigan. She fell in love with country living almost instantly.

Kathy credits her mother, who is also an artist, for her interest in art. As a child, Kathy busily sculpted animals out of soap, and later wood, while her mother painted landscapes and people. High school and college art classes intensified her interest in art and sculpture. She started sculpting clay animals in a ceramics class in college. Fellow students were soon asking Kathy to create animals for them. Kathy graduated Magna Cum Laude with an Associates Degree in Commercial Art.

Working out of her parent's home, Kathy started selling her one-of-a-kind animal sculptures at art fairs and shows. Soon she was supplying over 70 stores including the Mole Hole, a nationwide chain of collectible gift stores.

In 1983, Gene Freedman (then President of Enesco Corp.) first saw Kathy's work in a Seattle gift shop. This man, who launched Precious Moments, saw potential in Kathy's art and contacted her to start the first of her many lines in the giftware industry. Over the years, Kathy has designed and sculpted over one thousand different items in over forty lines that have been sold worldwide.

In the early 90s, Kathy sculpted realistic wildlife figures which were cast in bronze. At Detroit's Center for the Creative Arts, she learned the entire bronze casting process. Kathy's bronzes have been displayed in art galleries in Arizona and Michigan.

In her art career, Kathy has worked in both two and three dimensional media including clay, stone and wood. She first began designing intarsia patterns for her father-in-law over 13 years ago. When one of his customers would ask for a hard-to-find dog breed, or wanted a special custom intarsia of their pet, Kathy would create the pattern. She realized there was a demand for her unique intarsia patterns and now has over 300 patterns and a devoted following. Each pattern has a unique personality that is not found in other intarsia patterns currently available.

In Fall of 2004, *Scroll Saw Woodworking and Crafts* (Fox Chapel Publishing) published the first article by Kathy Wise, featuring her Boston Terrier intarsia design and step-by-step instructions. Kathy is now a regular contributor to the magazine and her work has been featured on several covers. Along with new patterns, articles, DVDs and beginner kits, Kathy creates custom intarsia murals and is currently working on her second book. Kathy Wise lives in Michigan with her two daughters, Sarah and Stacy, and husband Larry Brennan.

REARING PAINT STALLION #614 OS

Jaguar Jungle (2,072 pieces, 56" x 35") won 1st in Intarsia, Best in Scollsaw, and 2nd for the Peoples' Choice award at the highly acclaimed Design in Wood show in Del Mar, CA.

KATHY WISE DESIGNS, INC.

With over 300 beautiful and unique intarsia pattern designs available, you will be sure to find the pattern design you want. Kathy Wise Designs has the largest selection of dog-breed intarsia offered anywhere.

Choose from:

Horses	Birds	170 Dogs
Cats	Bears	Christmas Patterns
Puppies	Wildlife	Piece Patterns
Southwest	Intarsia Kits	Beginner Patterns
Landscapes	Hats/T-Shirts	

All Regular Patterns are $10

Oversized Patterns are $20

Intarsia Kits are $20 + shipping

Buy 5 patterns and get the next one free ($8.33 each)

Visit www.KathyWise.com to see the latest catalog or send $1 to receive a catalog by mail. You will also receive a coupon for $1 off your first catalog order.

Kathy Wise Designs
PO Box 60, Yale, MI 48097, Fax: 810-387-9044
KathyWise@bignet.net, www.KathyWise.com

IRIS KIT
INCLUDES: WOOD, STEP BY STEP INSTRUCTIONS, PATTERNS AND HANGERS.

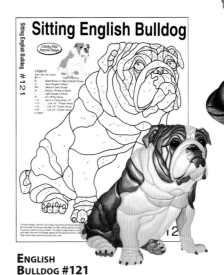

ENGLISH BULLDOG #121

GOLDEN RETRIEVER PUP #229

More Great Books from Fox Chapel Publishing

Easy to Make Inlay Wood Projects Intarsia
By Judy Gale Roberts and Jerry Booher
Learn to make a dozen beautiful inlay projects with all varieties of wood—from poplar to walnut.
$19.95
ISBN 978-1-56523-126-9

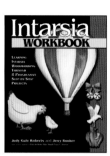

Intarsia Workbook
By Judy Gale Roberts and Jerry Booher
Master the stunningly beautiful and timeless art of intarsia with this skill-building manual from an award-winning artist.
$14.95
ISBN 978-1-56523-226-6

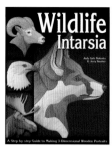

Wildlife Intarsia
By Judy Gale Roberts and Jerry Booher
Go wild for 14 sensational portrait patterns! Includes step-by-step instructions for a bald eagle, wild mustang & bull moose.
$19.95
ISBN 978-1-56523-282-2

Animal Puzzles for the Scroll Saw, 2nd Edition, Revised and Expanded
By Judy and Dave Peterson
Now with 50 patterns for creating fascinating free-standing puzzles of your furry and feathered friends.
$17.95
ISBN 978-1-56523-391-1

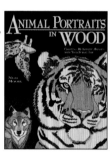

Animal Portraits in Wood
By Neal Moore
16 precisely designed and color-coded patterns for creating stunning segmented portraiture on your scroll saw.
$17.95
ISBN 978-1-56523-293-8

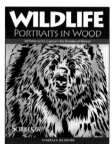

Wildlife Portraits in Wood
By Charles Dearing
Captures beautiful & fascinating wildlife scenery from around the world. 30 attractive patterns to adorn your home.
$14.95
ISBN 978-1-56523-338-6

Learn from the Experts

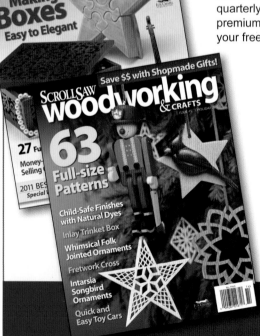

You already know that Fox Chapel Publishing is a leading source for woodworking books, videos, and DVDs, but did you know that we also publish *Scroll Saw Woodworking & Crafts*? Published quarterly, *Scroll Saw Woodworking & Crafts* is the magazine scroll saw enthusiasts turn to for the premium projects and expert information from today's leading wood crafters. Contact us today for your free trial issue!

ScrollSaw woodworking & CRAFTS

- Written by today's leading scroll saw artists
- Dozens of attractive, shop-tested patterns and project ideas for scrollers of all skill levels
- Great full-color photos of step-by-step projects and completed work—presented in a clear, easy-to-follow format
- Keep up with what's new in the scrolling community with tool reviews, artist profiles, and event coverage

Subscribe Today! 888-840-8590 • www.scrollsawer.com

Only $19.95 per year/4 issues! By mail, please send check or money order to:
Scroll Saw Woodworking & Crafts, 1970 Broad Street, East Petersburg, PA 17520

Look for These Books at Your Local Bookstore or Specialty Retailer

To order direct, call **800-457-9112** or visit *www.FoxChapelPublishing.com*
By mail, please send check or money order + S&H to:
Fox Chapel Publishing, 1970 Broad Street, East Petersburg, PA 17520

# Item	US Shipping Rate
1 Item	$3.99
Each Additional	.99

Canadian & International Orders – please email info@foxchapelpublishing.com or visit our website for actual shipping costs.